Follow Me Forward

A Practical Model for
Professional Learning
That Works

Hope Reagan
Alice Oakley

ISBN paperback 978-1-965438-14-5
ISBN ebook 978-1-965438-15-2
Published by Soro Publishing

For more information about our books and authors, visit our website: www.soropublishing.com.

Dedication

For Garrison, Katie, Miller & Lillian

You are our constant guiding lights, reminding us
that the path forward is brighter when we walk it together.
May you always have the courage to follow your
own light and the grace to shine it for others.

Table of Contents

Preface. vii

Introduction 1

Part 1:
Foundations for Professional Learning That Works

Chapter 1: Values That Enable Transformation. 17

Chapter 2: Beliefs That Shape Lasting Learning 33

Part 2:
Collaborative Learning Loops

Chapter 3: Phase 1: Create a Culture for Host Teachers. 51

Chapter 4: Phase 2: Build Capacity with Host Teachers 67

Chapter 5: Phase 3: Practice, Self-Reflect, and Polish 81

Chapter 6: Phase 4: Immerse in Practice 89

Chapter 7: Phase 5: Reflect and Reset. 99

Conclusion 109

Appendices. 113

    Appendix 1. Follow Me Forward Roles 114

    Appendix 2. Continuum of Practice Sample 115

    Appendix 3. Continuum of Practice with Feedback. 118

    Appendix 4. Collaborative Debrief Tool 122

    Appendix 5. What the Visit Is / What the Visit Is Not 124

References Cited 125

About the Authors. 127

Preface

Our Story of Discovery

IN THE FALL OF 2024, we became curious about designing an elevated model for professional learning. Over our twenty years in business, the Education Resource Group (ERG) team of coaches, including cofounders Hope and Alice, had coached countless teachers, shared numerous resources and tips, written page after page of feedback, and celebrated a host of accomplishments alongside schools. Yet something lingered. Too often, when ERG's coaching stopped, the application of learning seemed to stop, too.

As one ERG coach reflected, "I had a very fruitful coaching session… but then the next coaching session came, and it's like nothing really changed. We were back to the same conversation and the same feedback. I seriously began to wonder how much value my coaching is really bringing to the teacher."

We began to wonder: *What happened when we weren't in the classroom?*

Over the years, we had tested innovative approaches to address this question. We incorporated learning walks, where teachers observed each other briefly (five minutes), noting wows and wonders before moving on to the next class. This worked well to raise awareness and help people reflect and make time for important conversations around teaching and learning. We also developed leadership models, where school-level coaches shadowed our process and then gradually stepped in to "coach the coach." This was successful to build coaching capacity and increase the likelihood of implementation. Both of these models extended the work beyond our coaching visits. One principal noted, "When ERG equips our school-level coaches to carry on the work when you aren't in the building, we see more sustainability."

Still, the comment from the ERG coach stayed with us.

How could we enable learning that didn't pause when a coach left but lived in the very fabric of the school? Would it be possible to create professional development rooted in connected classrooms where teachers believed they could learn from each other while the leaders valued lifelong learning, authenticity, and belonging in the school culture? What was missing?

We began to consider a different kind of professional learning where teachers weren't just recipients of coaching but became leaders of it. What would need to happen to create confident teachers who open their doors, invite colleagues in, and influence other teachers directly from their own classrooms?

Those questions lingered, and from our pondering emerged an experiment.

The First Step

We reached out to a friend who was also an area superintendent in a large nearby school district. She had been an early champion of job-embedded professional learning (and had even written her dissertation on the successful implementation of job-embedded coaching). We expressed our concerns regarding coaching and its lack of implementation at times, despite having implemented job-embedded coaching with all the best practices in place. We also shared some new and innovative ideas and the values we were envisioning (lifelong learning, authenticity, and belonging) related to setting up host classrooms with teachers, for teachers. At the end of the conversation, she said, "If you're serious about this, I have a school that will be ready to try. The principal is innovative, and I believe she has teachers who are open to something different."

Soon after our conversation, we were in the media center of that elementary school, meeting with the second-grade team to discuss host classrooms that focused on their goal to make small-group instruction more productive. These teachers had expressed concerns about engagement during whole-group instruction, so this was an organic opportunity for these teachers to lead the initiative. We reassured these teachers: "This isn't about being perfect. It's about learning together. Who's willing to take a risk?"

Trial and Error

The work began with a grade-level learning opportunity on best practices for productive small-group instruction. In a follow-up session, an ERG consultant gathered the teachers around a kidney-shaped table while modeling small-group instruction.

"Notice how I'm checking for understanding here," she said, pointing to a student's work.

One teacher whispered, "It's so different actually seeing it with our kids, not just reading about it."

Next came a feedback support cycle. After the modeling of the productive small groups, support was provided to the second-grade teachers through observation and feedback.

A Spark Catches

One teacher wholeheartedly leaned into being a host classroom teacher. We asked if she would be willing to open her classroom to visiting peers, and she replied without hesitation, "If my struggles and successes help someone else, then absolutely come on in. It will be a privilege to work directly with my colleagues and inspire them to try new methods when delivering lessons to students within their own classrooms."

On the first observation day, five visiting teachers gathered outside her door. We reminded them, "Focus on the teaching and learning. Don't get distracted by chatting with students or looking at classroom decorations. Watch what the teacher does and how students respond."

Inside, this teacher moved with confidence, rotating groups and releasing responsibility to the students, asking questions that pushed her students to explain their thinking. One visitor commented, "I've never seen my students this engaged when I try small groups. I need to stop talking so much and start asking better questions."

After the classroom visit, we pulled chairs into an intimate circle in a small conference room. After some initial reflection about the visit, the host classroom teacher joined us.

One teacher began, "I noticed how you redirected without breaking the flow. How do you manage that?"

Another visitor chimed in, "Seeing it live just feels different. I'm already thinking of how to use this."

The conversation that unfolded between these educators was quite amazing.

The Discovery

After several months, more than twenty teachers had observed this host classroom. We began to reflect on what made this process so inspiring and made so much sense to us, teachers, and leaders. What struck us most wasn't just what visitors saw during the classroom visit but what they said afterward:

- "I finally understand how small groups can work."
- "I didn't just hear about a strategy; I saw it in action."
- "I want to try this with my own students tomorrow."
- "I have been doing everything wrong. Now I get it."
- "Something just feels good about learning from a peer."
- "This experience was inspiring."

The principal reflected, "When other teachers observe her in action and return to their own classrooms to implement what they've learned, that's when the real ripple effect happens… We are fully committed to doing whatever it takes to support student learning, and the [work anchored around this] host classroom is clearly making a powerful difference for *all* learners."

It became clear: the host classroom wasn't just a project. It was the beginning of a road map for a new way forward.

A New Way Forward

Looking back, the host classrooms were never just about supporting second-grade teachers with productive small-group instruction. They represented something much bigger than we realized at the time. They were about authentic learning in real classrooms, the transformative power of collaboration, and curious teachers having a say in what they wanted to learn more about. Teachers were proud of what they were doing and energized by the chance to share their practice. When colleagues stepped in to watch, it wasn't intimidating; it was affirming. Teachers, both visitors and host teachers, felt a renewed sense of belonging and purpose.

As our cooperating superintendent later reflected, "What happened with this experiment was amazing. When teachers start learning from each other and getting excited about what they are doing in authentic classroom settings, the sky is the limit. This is the type of experience that can set up teachers to take over their own learning. Instead of teaching being a means to an end, they become curious, and they study and research and learn on their own. They become motivated to learn just like we want our students to be."

From a Discovery to a Model

So how did this experience change our thinking about professional learning?

Like most professional development, our approach had focused more on changing teacher behaviors. While we could create initial changes in actions or behaviors, they did not always last when our work together came to a close. For example, on a regular basis, we work with leaders who want to see more small groups and less whole-group instruction. The leader typically asks what we can do to help them achieve their goal of supporting teacher behaviors around small-group work. We develop a proposal of action steps related to the goals of the project, including teacher and student behaviors. However, we had identified a missing piece. The behaviors and actions don't change in a lasting sustainable way until we consider our values and our beliefs.

Now, our thinking about professional learning is more holistic, constructive, and experiential. Instead of simply prescribing actions to change teacher behaviors, we support who teachers want to *be* and what they would *do* in their classrooms to make that vision come alive. For instance, through a process of reflection on values and beliefs, a group of teachers may determine, "We want to be teachers who know how to offer our students meaningful tasks, not isolated skill work that is never applied in real-world contexts." We can fully support this organic aspiration of these teachers who believe meaningful work is important.

What we discovered became the values and beliefs of our new model, Follow Me Forward, and is simple yet profound:

- Lifelong learning and curiosity should be a priority.
- Authenticity can deepen collaboration with colleagues.
- Ultimately classrooms can be living, meaningful sanctuaries for learning where a sense of belonging is pervasive.

Introduction

The Need for Change

OUR PROFESSIONAL LEARNING SYSTEM IS broken. Currently, most professional learning is one dimensional, focused on compliance, and often disjointed. It is a disordered system that keeps teachers in a professional game of checking boxes and running from one mandate to the next. No say. No agency.

Because of this, many of our classrooms are no longer places of joy. Teachers are managing a thousand things they have been told to do. It is commonplace to shut down instruction for the required assessments, use worksheets that are not aligned with standards, place students on computer programs that are mandated but only slightly encourage critical thinking, and rarely create authentic learning. Teachers are trying to be compliant but are often given competing priorities. When we talk to teachers, they say they love students, and many self report a love of actual teaching. But something is missing. Everyone is busy, but the instruction often lacks meaning and certainly lacks alignment. Over the years, states and districts have added more things to do but are reluctant to remove anything. No wonder the bubble has burst. There is a lack of motivation to keep learning, no clear sense of purpose, and a growing feeling of isolation. These feelings are pervasive when it comes to professional learning as well.

For example, let's consider Jane. Jane started teaching a few years ago. She loves the work and the students but has not had access to effective professional learning. Jane is compliant but is not internalizing new initiatives. She feels like she is falling short when people observe and give her more to do without considering her immediate needs. Jane craves useful feedback but feels a disconnect with her day-to-day demands and professional learning experiences. She is reluctant to try new things because she cannot see how to implement them even though she has a basic understanding and has considered them. Year after year, Jane continues to teach and attend meetings, and she starts to become cynical. She quietly tunes out in meetings and brings other work to do instead of paying attention. She knows her needs are not being met, and she expects the meetings to be a waste of her time. Jane goes into her classroom and does the best she can but knows something is missing. She quietly disengages herself as a lifelong learner and begins to follow manuals and programs that are available. Jane no longer contributes collaboratively or authentically because she cannot see the point in doing more for possibly less results.

Jane's principal knows she needs to support Jane (and others like her) but does not know how to in the midst of all the demands in schools. With all the other things to do, her principal asks the instructional support facilitator to help. The facilitator is fresh out of the classroom, and although she is an expert in content, she is not equipped to teach other adults to learn. She is highly motivated to help others, gives extensive resources, and creates polished presentations. Unfortunately, the resources and presentations do not get used, and her scheduled meetings result in people nodding in agreement but few meaningful results. Conversations in these meetings often digress into complaints about students and rut stories. No real solutions are offered, and everyone goes back to their classrooms with a sense of dread. Jane is frustrated and does not feel a sense of belonging. Her principal is overwhelmed, and the instructional facilitator begins to become cynical because change is not happening no matter how many resources are shared. Then this cycle continues.

The characters in this example may be familiar. If we do not change our course with professional learning, we can all end up like Jane, the principal, or the instructional facilitator.

Problems with Current Professional Learning

Professional learning is meant to improve instruction and ultimately student outcomes. The Harvard Graduate School of Education (2023) reports that school districts around the country spend an estimated $18 billion on teacher learning programs. Yet, most teachers show little to no sustained improvement with only about 30 percent demonstrating substantial and sustained gains over multiple years (TNTP, 2015).

Visits to classrooms underscore this finding. Teachers often tell us that they are used to getting "one more thing" put on their plate at the beginning of each year. They associate professional learning initiatives with new leaders, political trends, or board mandates. There is a sense that professional learning is done "to" them instead of "with" them. Typically, traditional models of professional development fall short in creating meaningful and lasting change for educators and students. This results in several unintended consequences.

Consequence 1: Recruiting and Retention Problems

A lack of quality learning opportunities and ongoing support in initiatives creates a recruiting and retention problem. Even with conservative estimates, Nguyen et al (2024) show tens of thousands of vacancies and nearly 300,000 underqualified hires, which impact one in ten classroom positions. This underscores an ongoing strain on teacher recruitment and staffing. One study (Cells, et al 2023) found that key factors in whether teachers stayed in the profession beyond the five-year mark included levels of support such as professional development, opportunities for growth, time to collaborate with colleagues, and autonomy. In fact, the study showed teachers who reported substantial professional support were more likely to stay while lack of professional support was tied to attrition. Connor et al (2024) found that teachers with ongoing support over time were twice as likely to improve instruction compared with those who only attended isolated workshops. Without quality professional learning, teachers leave their roles and lifelong learning will not exist in our classrooms.

Consequence 2: Low Impact on Student Learning

Additionally, professional learning often focuses on skills and knowledge but often misses opportunities to create real, lasting change with teachers and students. A 2025 review of 46 studies found that professional learning focused only on knowledge and skills made little impact on student learning (Hill & Papay, 2025). Alternatively, the study showed that linking professional learning directly to classroom practices led to teacher improvement that resulted in higher student outcomes compared to generic training sessions. When we don't provide authentic and relevant professional learning opportunities, teachers and students suffer.

Consequence 3: Resistance

The current practices around professional learning often hyper-focus on outcomes without considering context. We often gather large groups of educators in rooms and "teach" them the same thing because they "all need to be on the same page." This practice is outdated and is often a demotivating factor for the best and brightest teachers who already understand the content, initiative, or mandate.

In addition, teachers who only learn to read manuals or follow scripts as part of district initiatives report reduced autonomy and less engagement. This approach ignores backgrounds, individual experiences, and unique expertise. In fact, a study of over 5,000 students found that collaborative professional learning formats tailored to teacher needs resulted in 25 percent more math progress in 8 months (Gore et al, 2024). The study went on to show that personalized, embedded professional development models improved teacher performance across the board as opposed to everyone getting the same thing. When teachers cannot see themselves in the work and are left out of the process, there is less engagement and more resistance. Collaboration becomes nonexistent, and curiosity and meaning, two drivers of change, are extinguished.

We do not see the current problems in this section as professional growth or development, but rather as sources of frustration and dread for educators. For this reason, we use the term *professional learning* instead of *professional development*. Learning is at the heart of the *Follow Me Forward* work. The model is not just another framework or a train-the-trainer structure. Instead, what we offer is an elevated model of professional learning that actually works, designed to transform educators from the inside out.

What Is Needed: A New Model

Traditional professional support usually takes one of two forms. The first is the familiar "sit-and-get" model, where everyone receives the same information at the same time and is expected to progress from a single starting point. This ignores the reality that teachers have diverse experiences and needs, so starting in the same place is impossible.

The second form, job-embedded coaching, has improved on this approach but still faces challenges. Too often, success depends heavily on the coach's skills and capacity. When coaches are stretched thin or lack expertise in specific areas, growth stalls. Without true collaboration or awareness of individual bias, even well-intended coaching can fall short.

Follow Me Forward offers a new, better model, one that enables meaningful growth and lasting change. It's built for educators who value lifelong learning, authenticity, and community. Grounded in curiosity, collaboration, and meaning, it blends the best attributes of workshops and coaching while creating a sense of belonging among teachers. Educators deserve professional growth that honors who they *are*, not just what they *do.* Andragogy is emphasized over pedagogy. Teachers who remain reflective and open to learning throughout their careers are essential to student success, yet too many are burning out due to poor professional support.

Follow Me Forward creates the conditions educators need to thrive and leads the way toward a new era of professional learning.

The Follow Me Forward Model

Follow Me Forward introduces the only professional learning model that immerses teachers in real-time, real-world growth by learning from one another within the school day instead of outside of it. This model replaces passive and redundant meetings and workshops with an active learning ecosystem, where teachers set goals, receive personalized support, observe peers, and reflect collaboratively while grounded in what works best for adult learners. This model elevates the typical job-embedded coaching cycle to a whole-school continuous learning model. The goal is not compliance, but instead, transformation.

The Follow Me Forward Model is a dynamic approach to professional learning and is multi-dimensional. It combines the invisible and internal work of values and beliefs with the visible and external work of implementing learning loops. It is holistic and takes into account not only the desired results of professional learning, but the humans within it. This is not a linear process that a person begins and ends. Instead, it is a professional learning experience that puts educators on the path to a lasting professional metamorphosis.

Values. Each of us holds a system of values based on our unique life experiences. The values within a professional learning model need to align with the beliefs and also drive the external behaviors we see in schools. In the Follow Me Forward Model, we prioritize the values of lifelong learning, authenticity, and belonging throughout each phase. These values drive the beliefs we hold and are the foundation for our actions.

Beliefs. What we believe determines the kind of person we want to be. It is vital we attend to our beliefs in a professional learning model because what individuals believe will drive behaviors and actions related to professional learning. If we value lifelong learning, authenticity, and belonging, then we believe in curiosity, collaboration, and meaning. The results of professional learning are not separate from the individuals within it. Because of this, we intentionally address beliefs as an important component of the work.

Learning Loops. The five phases of the Follow Me Forward Model are concrete and actionable, so they become ongoing learning loops. What makes them unique is that they are not only focused on the impact of professional learning on students, but they are also designed to reflect the values and beliefs set forth in the Follow Me Forward Model for building teacher capacity. The learning loops are designed to be continuous, so the work builds on itself each year.

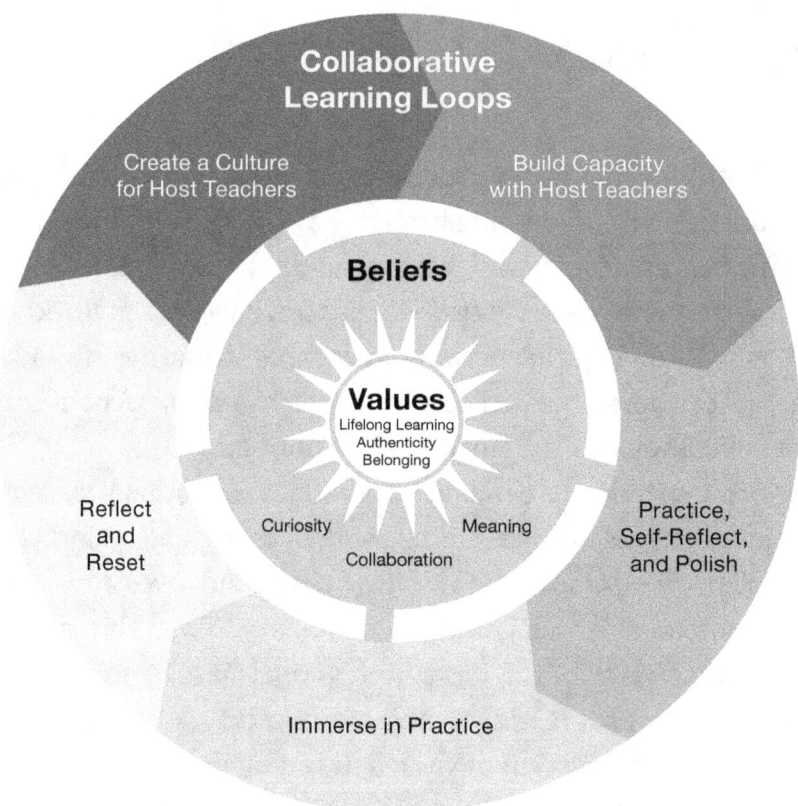

Sustainable Change in Professional Learning

One of the biggest challenges in professional development is sustaining change. Kurt Lewin's (1947) change theory helps explain why. He proposed that lasting change moves through three stages: unfreezing, changing, and refreezing.

- **Unfreezing:** In the unfreezing stage, leaders help staff recognize the need for change and loosen old habits or beliefs.
- **Changing:** The changing stage introduces and tests new ideas and practices.
- **Refreezing:** Finally, the refreezing stage stabilizes those new practices, so they become part of the school culture.

True change, Lewin argued, reshapes both behavior *and* mindset.

Too often, schools skip the unfreezing stage and jump straight to new programs or fixes. When teachers don't understand *why* change is needed or haven't released outdated assumptions, new initiatives rarely take hold. Effective leaders stay in the unfreezing stage long enough to build readiness before moving forward. Ignoring any stage, especially the first, sets even the best ideas up for failure, a mistake reflected in the 70 percent of change efforts that don't last (Anderson, 2020).

The typical professional development initiative in schools looks something like this:

Ineffective Professional Learning Approach		
Lewin Phase	**Learning Timeline**	**Results**
1: Unfreezing	Skipped	• Ill-defined problem • Unclear vision • Additions instead of replacements
2: Changing	Fall	• Lack of engagement • Confusion • Overwhelmed participants • Abandoning and resistance
3: Refreezing	Winter/Spring	• Failed initiatives • Angry and cynical participants

A more effective professional learning model is as follows:

Effective Professional Learning Approach		
Lewin Phase	Learning Timeline	Results
1: Unfreezing	Spring/ Summer	• Collaborative conversations • New vision creating need for change • Replacement of old behaviors and ideas
2: Changing	Fall	• Rapid forward movement • Curious and engaged adult learners • Growth of individuals
3: Refreezing	Winter/Spring	• Reinforcement of new behaviors • Celebrations of success • Eagerness to learn more

The Follow Me Forward Model builds on Lewin's change theory by guiding educators through each phase of growth.

- To support **unfreezing**, teachers begin by reflecting on current practices, identifying gaps, and clarifying shared visions and goals.
- The **changing** phase happens through collaboration when teachers experiment with new strategies, engage in coaching, and learn alongside peers.
- To support **refreezing**, those new practices become part of daily instruction, supported by structures for reflection and shared responsibility.

By connecting Lewin's (1947) framework to the Follow Me Forward Model, schools can turn professional learning into an ongoing cycle that builds capacity, ownership, and lasting improvement.

Moving from an Event to an Experience

In addition to Lewin's theory, the Follow Me Forward Model for professional learning rests on values and beliefs that drive internal motivation. Unlike one-shot workshops or even coaching cycles that depend on a single individual's capacity, this model creates systems of sustainability that are embedded in the school culture. Professional learning becomes a human-to-human experience rather than one or more isolated events.

This shift in design matters for three reasons:

- **The model builds capacity.** Participants develop transferable leadership skills that travel with them across schools and districts and stay with them in current roles.
- **The model is sustainable.** Learning stays in the classroom and the building. It is not dependent on external trainers or temporary initiatives. The expertise is built from within.
- **The model creates collective responsibility.** Teachers, Support Leaders, visitors, and consultants (when utilized) share ownership of the work across their roles, so no one carries it alone.

It is important to note the Follow Me Forward Model features a cyclical five-phase Learning Loop process across one school year. At first glance, the phases may appear to be linear in nature. However, they are actually circular and cyclical, so the participants move through the phases and then begin again. This is a significant difference in the Follow Me Forward Model when compared to other professional learning models. *Follow Me Forward* is not just about a destination or a result. The Follow Me Forward Model enables transformation for the individuals who are on a collaborative path to lasting change. Through our fieldwork, we have witnessed this process bring humanity back to the center of professional learning.

An Overview of This Book

Part I: Foundations for Professional Learning That Works reveals the important and invisible work of values and beliefs. This portion of the book is devoted to the multidimensional idea of *being* and *doing* and how transformational professional learning impacts the larger instructional culture within a school.

- **Chapter 1: Values That Enable Transformation** explores the origin of the Follow Me Forward Model along with how traditional professional learning falls short. This chapter addresses the values of lifelong learning, authenticity, and belonging and makes the case for why these are keys to successful and sustainable professional learning.
- **Chapter 2: Beliefs That Shape Lasting Learning** describes the gaps in current professional learning models and how principles of adult learning can address them. The three beliefs of the Follow Me Forward Model that drive motivation and engagement are introduced as curiosity, collaboration, and meaning. The link between these beliefs and transformational adult learning is explained and solidified in this chapter.

Part 2: Collaborative Learning Loops lead you through the specific actions of this model, showing how the values, beliefs, and Learning Loops work together. These phases are cyclical, so that participants find themselves back at Phase 1 at the completion of Phase 5.

- **Chapter 3: Phase 1: Create a Culture for Host Teachers** emphasizes the selection of a Support Leader as the critical first step of all the phases. After the Support Leader is in place, you'll learn how to set the stage for professional learning taking into account the values and beliefs of the Follow Me Forward Model. The team sets instructional goals collaboratively and develops a Continuum of Practice. In addition, you will learn how to intentionally invite two to four teachers to be Host Teachers.
- **Chapter 4: Phase 2: Build Capacity with Host Teachers** shows the Support Leader how to deliver content through learning opportunities and demonstration lessons for the Host Teachers, ways to support the Host Teachers, and the importance of strength-based feedback.
- **Chapter 5: Phase 3: Practice, Self-Reflect, and Polish** is the phase to gradually release the Host Teacher. The Host Teachers immerse themselves in practice, re-

flection, and polishing ideas from the Continuum of Practice. Host Teachers also explicitly prepare for visitors. The Support Leader is in regular contact with the Host Teacher during this time and offers support as needed.

- **Chapter 6: Phase 4: Immerse in Practice** unpacks the components included when visitors are welcomed into the Host Classrooms for collaborative learning. The Support Leader intentionally and strategically prepares visitors before, during, and after the visit to ensure success for building capacity for all learners.
- **Chapter 7: Phase 5: Reflect and Reset** explores the critical role this phase plays in the transformational process of not ending but rather making the commitment to scale the phases in a *loop*. This phase emphasizes the power of professional reflection. Importance is placed on utilizing reflections to determine relevant and actionable next steps.

Case Studies

Each of the chapters in Part 2 will bring you alongside elementary, middle, and high school educator teams who've engaged in this work. By sharing case studies, we have created a way to help you see and hear how this work takes shape in real schools. These examples are not meant to portray perfection because we know that does not exist. Instead, the case studies help you see what is possible with the Follow Me Forward Model. Each case study illustrates implementation, showing how the model looks in practice at different levels and within unique contexts. Below, you will find contextual information about each of the schools. The names of the schools and teachers involved in the work have been changed, but they are real. The goal is for you, the reader, to see what is possible.

- All of the case study schools mentioned are part of a public school district in the United States. The district is large and diverse, with over 50,000 students spread across eighty schools in urban and suburban communities.
- The elementary case studies take place in Franklin Elementary, which is one of over forty elementary schools in the district. Franklin Elementary serves a diverse student population of over 700 students that reflect a wide range of backgrounds and learning needs.
- The middle school case studies are from West End Middle School, which is one of fifteen middle schools across the district and includes over 700 students. Many students at this school may face increased academic risk due to a combination of

their family's economic circumstances, language barriers, and prior educational experiences.

- Bailey High School is one of sixteen high schools in the district and serves over 1,700 students. It is particularly diverse in terms of countries of origin, race, and socioeconomic status.

Appendices

As part of the development of the Follow Me Forward Model, we created useful resources that support implementation. Some artifacts and examples are provided in the text and also included at the back of this book for easy access.

Bonus Resources

In addition to these appendices, Bonus Resources to support the Follow Me Forward Model can be accessed on our website www.myedresource.com.

Summary

The current professional learning systems are not able to meet the modern needs of teachers and students. Recruiting and retention suffer when the professional opportunities are lacking in quality and student impact falls short. In addition, resistance to initiatives can erode engagement and sustainability.

The Follow Me Forward Model offers a different solution unlike other professional models—one that can lead to lasting learning and sustainable change. Instead of putting content at the center of the work, it addresses learning in a holistic way. By starting from the inside out, participants align values, beliefs and actions over time. The Follow Me Forward Model integrates curiosity, collaboration, and meaningful work, so participants can experience lifelong learning, authenticity and belonging.

This elevated model builds on the workshops and coaching models that were created before it. With clear and actionable phases, participants engage in learning loops that weave in the values and belief systems while supporting the participants each step of the way.

Building on Lewin's Change Theory (1947), this model emphasizes the need to unfreeze, change, and refreeze in the context of professional learning. In short, the model transforms professional learning from a fleeting event into a sustainable, transformational experience.

PART 1

Foundations for Professional Learning That Works

CHAPTER 1

Values That Enable Transformation

EARLY IN HER CAREER, ALICE attended a writing workshop for teachers. The materials were attractive and packaged in a spiral resource book that was ready for easy copying. They included test prep drills related to grammar and punctuation. At first glance, her task was simple: finish the training, go back to her school, and utilize the materials. She also inherently knew she did not need to question or complain. This was a district mandate, and the decisions had already been made regarding what would happen, when it would happen, and how. However, what was not so simple was that her picture of quality teaching did not align with the materials. Alice valued authentic learning experiences and understood that people learn by doing. Writing was no exception. In order to become excellent writers, her students needed to write. She could support the isolated skills work in a variety of ways, but she firmly believed writing should be an authentic expression of self, shaping ideas into meaning instead of simply circling prepositions or writing to prompts for a test.

This tension pulled Alice in two directions. On one side, she wanted to follow the rules of her school, district, and state and not rock the boat. On the other side, she had conviction for what students should be experiencing as writers. She wanted to meet the expectations of her school and district, but she could not ignore the fact that the worksheets chipped away at the very heart of learning. So she made a quiet choice. She closed her classroom door, slid the resource manual into the cabinet, and did not pull it back out. Instead, she had students immersed in authentic writing to include stories, essays, and reflections that mattered to them. On the outside, nothing looked different. On the inside, she was aligning her values with her teaching.

The Problem

Most professional development approaches work from the outside in. External factors such as administrators, school boards, or legislators tell teachers what they need to know and be able to do, and on a good day, they sometimes explain why. The problem with this top-down approach is that it positions teachers as passive recipients rather than active participants in their growth. When learning is prescribed without genuine teacher input, it often feels disconnected from classroom realities. Initiatives are rolled out in one-size-fits-all workshops that rarely address the diverse needs of teachers or the unique challenges of their students. This creates a sense of compliance rather than commitment, leaving many educators feeling that professional development is something "done to them" instead of "created with them." As a result, even well-intentioned programs often fail to produce meaningful or lasting change, contributing to the cycle of frustration, burnout, and disengagement in schools.

What Is Needed: Being and Doing

Our Follow Me Forward Model works on the core concept that teachers are intrinsically motivated. They have a unique view of the world based on lived experiences, and their agency comes from within. Change also originates from within them and not outside them. The Follow Me Forward Model is one that does not prescribe *what* to do; rather it helps educators determine who they want to be within the professional learning experience based on values. The Follow Me Forward Model is designed to promote the values of lifelong learning, authenticity, and belonging.

William Powers' *Perceptual Control Theory* (1973) suggests that human behavior is driven by our need for internal balance. He says we all have a picture in our minds of how things should be based on our experiences, values, and beliefs. When real life doesn't match that picture, we try to fix it. We do this either by changing our behavior or by redefining our goal. True control comes from within, as we continually seek balance between what we do and who we want to be.

In schools, this means student behavior is not random. It is purposeful even if it is unconscious. Each student acts in ways that help them maintain their own sense of balance and identity. For example, a student who believes they're "not smart" may avoid tasks or act out to protect that self-image. Their behavior helps them regain perceived control, even if it leads to negative outcomes. In contrast, a student who sees themselves as capable and growing may demonstrate that belief through actions such as participating in class and completing work. For educators, understanding this framework shifts our approach from managing behavior to helping students reshape the way they see themselves as learners.

The same truth applies to adults in professional learning. An educator may appear resistant to new practices not because of laziness but because they cannot yet perceive themselves as successful in using them. All behavior is purposeful. If we want lasting growth, we must consider not only what we want to *do* as it relates to professional learning, but also who we want to *be*.

Our values drive our beliefs.
Our beliefs drive our actions.
Our actions make our values and beliefs visible.

The Follow Me Forward Model is built on the powerful interplay between *being* (our values and beliefs) and *doing* (the visible actions that bring those inner qualities to life). Transformation occurs when these two dimensions align, when what we believe about teaching and learning is reflected in what we do each day. At its core, the Follow Me Forward Model is a value-based model designed to engage the whole educator. The values of lifelong learning, authenticity, and belonging serve as guiding lights that shape identity and purpose, while the beliefs of curiosity, collaboration, and meaning flow naturally from them. Through the five phases of the Learning Loop, these values and beliefs are translated into tangible, observable practices. In this alignment of being and doing, professional learning evolves from isolated events into a living cycle of inquiry, reflection, and growth. The result is not just compliance or even improved practice, but lasting transformation.

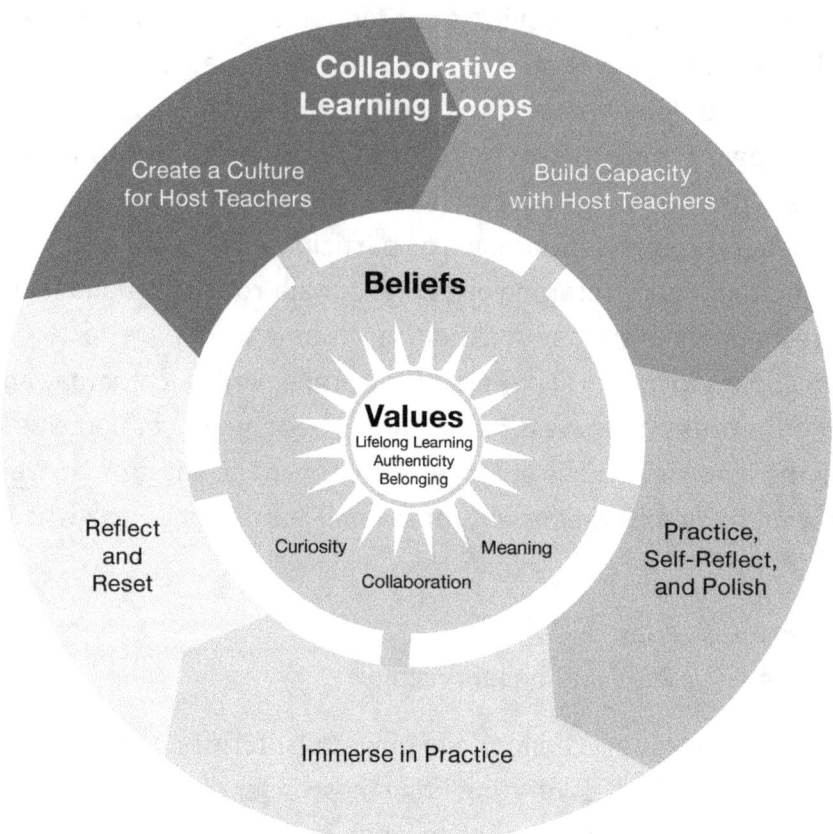

Values

The guiding lights of the Follow Me Forward Model is a shared system of values that shapes both who we are as educators and how we work together. We center the professional learning system on three core values: lifelong learning, authenticity, and belonging. These values are not simply words or part of a mission statement, but instead are the compass for every decision, conversation, and practice within the model. When professional learning is grounded in a commitment to continual growth, honesty of practice, and creating spaces where every person is seen, heard, and valued, the result is a school culture where these values are visible in both our identity (*being*) and actions (*doing*).

By asking ourselves simple questions around being *and* doing, we can become our best selves as educators while honoring the values of the Follow Me Forward Model:

- What do I believe as a professional?

- What am I doing as a professional?
- Is it working? Is there a match between what I believe and what I am doing?
- What is the next step to move toward my best self as an educator?

For example, if we want to be educators who believe in authenticity but continue to purchase worksheets that are not meaningful for our work or our students, we can reflect on how this is working. It isn't. At least not working very well toward being our best educator selves. Perhaps the next step is to have a conversation with a colleague to find out what they are doing or trade a store-bought resource for one that is handmade and matches student needs.

Another example is administrators who say they want to see students immersed in authentic learning opportunities when they come into classrooms but continue to purchase technology or gimmicks that actually limit deep thinking and learning. When we reflect on how this is working, the next steps naturally emerge. Reducing classroom screen time and increasing the human time in active thinking and learning is one way to move toward more authentic learning experiences. This creates alignment and moves the dial toward our best selves as educators.

A third example is when schools say they value collaboration, but professional learning is designed as "sit-and-get" because covering the content is more important (and faster) than ensuring understanding. By taking time to revisit our values, we can clearly confirm whether what we are doing is working or not.

This kind of work is transformational. It is not just about content delivery, timelines, check-ins, or evaluations. It is about how our values shape how we show up in classrooms and as professionals. It impacts all facets of our practice.

The work at this value level is deep and abstract. It is unseen, often unnoticed, and can move slowly. Traditional professional development models often demand quick actions that can be misunderstood and overgeneralized upon execution. They often focus on what teachers are doing without any consideration of their internal values. Do they value the initiatives? Do they understand the initiative? Where do they enter into the initiative? The Follow Me Forward Model immerses participants in classrooms with Host Teachers, so this important internal work can take root. It encourages change from within.

This holistic, experiential approach integrates the Follow Me Forward values as well as driving beliefs that lead to concrete actionable steps in learning loops. The result is a professional learning model that is grounded in values and motivational research and creates an elevated professional learning experience that is sustainable for teachers and schools. When teachers and leaders use the following values as their foundation for change, their mindset shifts from asking, "Why?" to asking, "Why not?"

Lifelong Learning

Professional Learning Today

In recent years, we have observed a sad but obvious trend with lifelong learning. Simply put, educators do not want to do it. They have essentially raised their hands and said, "No more."

In many schools the lack of importance placed on lifelong learning shows up in required professional learning that is shallow, fragmented, and compliance driven. Teachers are resistant because they expect surface-level workshops that are perceived as irrelevant or to be told how to do "this one thing" without support to grow deep knowledge and expertise over time. Worse, some experiences have reduced educators to being a cog in a wheel by moving them through scripted programs or pre-packaged lessons instead of trusted professional decision-makers. The result is often resistance, skepticism, and disengagement. Unfortunately, these experiences have minimal impact on student learning.

The What and Why of Lifelong Learning

By contrast, the Follow Me Forward Model positions lifelong learning as a value. It reframes and redefines professional growth as continuous learning cycles. It reminds us that our lives and our teaching are not static. Instead, growth is not only a luxury but also a necessity and drives us closer to our best selves as educators. When teachers, administrators, and support staff engage in meaningful and connected learning, it is possible to rediscover the joy that once drew them into education. It is important to note that just because we have logged hours in education or have a way we have "always done it" does not mean we are done learning. We are never done. In fact, lifelong learning is a tool to highlight professional agency and shows that expertise matters. Educators are not just recipients of mandates, but active, engaging participants who can shape teaching and learning. In the Follow Me Forward Model, lifelong learning is both a mindset and mechanism that drives continual growth and builds self efficacy. This value can spark educators' curiosity and become embedded in a school culture.

How Lifelong Learning Guides Professional Learning

Mistakes are part of learning. Instead of teachers feeling like time is being wasted on professional learning, we want teachers and leaders to feel empowered, engaged, and part of the larger system for learning. The value of lifelong learning is one that can save us from dismal days. In schools and classrooms where lifelong learning is valued, the focus shifts from perfection to progress. This subtle shift allows room for mistakes.

We believe it is okay to make mistakes.

An important component of lifelong learning is what happens *after* the mistake. That is the magical place where learning can take root. If we expect teachers and leaders to be perfect, they limit their risk-taking. We know that risk-taking is an important principle in adult learning and a key component in transforming how people see themselves in the world (Mezirow, 1978). When people fear mistakes will be punished, risk-taking is limited, and they become stagnant. They can become melancholy. They become underwhelmed and bored and lack motivation.

Alternatively, when lifelong learning is valued, mistakes can be celebrated as thresholds to new skills, beliefs, understandings, and values. When we observe teachers, we look for the liminal space that is slightly beyond what people are already mastering, so they can stretch into the new spaces of learning. Vygotsky (1978) calls this the *zone of proximal development*. This is the place between what people already know and are able to do independently and what people are able to do with guidance and support. If we never dip into those places, we will rarely make mistakes. That might feel safe. However, if we always play it safe, we will rarely grow.

For example, a common pitfall in many classrooms is too much teacher talk and not enough student time spent in meaningful work. In order to curb this, a teacher who is a lifelong learner will notice this about themself, seek solutions, and then try them. The solutions might not all work, but giving oneself permission to make mistakes along the way creates agency and propels the adult learner forward. In the process, the teacher will most likely land on a solution (like setting a timer to stop the teacher talking), and this new learning becomes part of the teacher's professional evolution.

Leaders and Teachers as Learners

Another reason that lifelong learning is a core value of the Follow Me Forward Model is that beliefs around learning shape instructional practices. Debra Crouch (2022), drawing on Cambourne's Conditions of Learning, emphasizes that a teacher's beliefs about people's ability to learn can enable or constrain how we respond to them. The same holds true for our school leaders. If we take this one step further, we can reflect on ourselves.

What do we believe about our own learning?

If we are limited in our own ability to synthesize and learn across our professional lives, won't that impact our instructional work and decision making?

When we link this value of lifelong learning back to the Being/Doing model of William Powers, it is integral. Valuing lifelong learning is something that will be reflected in the actions we choose to take. When we see people committed to this value, we see the opposite of one-and-done professional learning. We see ongoing, job-embedded communities of learning that include high-quality conversations around goals, practices, feedback, and appropriate adjustments.

The Follow Me Forward Model is designed so this value of lifelong learning is emphasized throughout the Learning Loops. Taking time to choose a supportive leader who can guide teachers in reflecting on their values and beliefs is important. This support leader should also assist and support the continuum of practice as part of the invitation to open classrooms to visitors. They provide ongoing support throughout the process for the Host Teachers. Peers are then invited to learn alongside Host Teachers in real classrooms with real students. This approach makes clear that everyone is learning together, and the joy springs from this process, not just the outcomes.

When we take time to reflect on what we believe about our own learning, we can find out-dated ideas that might need to be dusted off. "I am not good at math" is something we often hear from adults in professional learning conversations, and we need to notice and note this kind of thinking. If we hold these comments as fact, then our actions around this value will align with not being good in math. Perhaps we don't put time and energy into learning it because we get overloaded or have a nagging feeling that takes us back to our elementary classrooms of anxiety around learning math. The accumulation of missed learning opportunities ends up sabotaging our math expertise, not our ability to learn. The value of lifelong learning within the Follow Me Forward Model helps us reframe this thinking. We can release the idea that we are not good at something. Not being proficient in math is not actually who we are. It is not our full identity. In fact, we can decide that we may not be good yet and can get better.

This same idea rings true for our Support Leaders and administration teams. If they are able to embrace the value of learning across a lifetime, then their views around professional development shift. They are not needed to supervise compliance; instead, they become true scaffolds, mentors, and facilitators of new learning. They are humble enough to engage in growth alongside their teachers. In contrast, leaders who do not value lifelong learning often believe that their staff is limited in what they know and are able to do. This shows up in their own decision-making when they cancel collaborative planning sessions in order to squeeze in more test-prep meetings. They limit opportunities because they assume people will not want to learn or will struggle too much with application. Instead of modeling curiosity or growth, their actions indicate that ongoing adult learning is secondary to compliance and short-term bandaids.

By orienting ourselves around the value of lifelong learning, we take full control of what is possible as learners. Focusing on lifelong learning as a value, we have created a professional learning system that is not just an event. We have created a system that is designed to be a never-ending learning loop that becomes a transformational experience.

Authenticity

Professional Learning Today

Current professional development has somewhat of an identity problem. Many times, we gather teachers to check boxes, encourage them to do the "dog and pony show" with visitors, or provide them with edutainment instead of meaningful professional learning experiences. We can sing and dance, hand out cute name tags and binders, and even bring in speakers with music and flair, but at the end of the day this does not mean practices will shift. Teachers complete the training but are not equipped with any tools. In addition, current professional development can be more about compliance rather than deep understanding of ideas. Initiatives are rolled out, checklists are put in place, classroom visits are made, and everyone carries on. In those spaces, we lose what matters most, which is helping educators grow in ways that are valuable and connected to the realities of their classrooms. The disconnect between districts and schools and classrooms is often ignored in the name of "fidelity," regardless of whether it applies to current instructional context.

Authenticity is the opposite of this. It is not being compliant for the sake of checking boxes or trying new practices just long enough to cross it off the list. These behaviors are counterproductive to true transformation. They erode trust and waste energy. Authentic professional learning asks educators to bring their real questions, struggles, and successes to the table. It expects educators to bring their whole self into the experience.

This is also important when we think about our leaders in schools. Many times, leaders try to show up as the absolute experts. They may have an underlying belief that they must be all-knowing to be a good leader. They tell teachers to "do better" without effective feedback on *how* to do better. Leaders may not understand specific instructional methods, so they find superficial things for people to work on to avoid revealing their own gaps in understanding. This is unfortunate because it is through vulnerability that our authenticity shines. Leaders can model this in a powerful way by acknowledging a mistake, sharing a personal story, identifying their own misconception about instructional methods, or having a hard but important conversation.

The What and Why of Authenticity

Authenticity is one of the core values of the Follow Me Forward Model because it provides guidance when we are put in challenging situations with teaching and learning. Brené Brown defines authenticity as "the daily practice of letting go of who we think we're supposed to be and embracing who we are." (Brown, 2010, p. 50) In education, this means that teachers, leaders, and students thrive when they act in alignment with their values, are willing to be seen, engage in honest reflection without fear of judgment, and bring their unique selves to the task. The Follow Me Forward Model is designed to make this kind of authenticity safe, visible, and doable.

Brené Brown's research reminds us that authenticity is a *practice*, not a fixed trait. Valuing authenticity requires daily choices to show up fully, even when it feels risky. In classrooms, this may mean a teacher admits to students, "I'm trying a new approach today, so let's see how it works." The value of authenticity drives the belief that they are confident professionals, and that drives the behaviors we see.

Across each Phase of Follow Me Forward Learning Loops, it is important that participants are authentic. We want teachers and leaders to be real. We do not want performances. When we value authenticity, we create collaborative sanctuaries for learning at all levels.

Joyful spaces. In practice, authenticity leads to joyful and safe spaces in our schools. In many cases, authenticity is what takes ordinary moments and makes them extraordinary because they are real, honest, and unfiltered. By focusing on being authentic, we can align our actions accordingly.

Follow Me Forward Story

One of the Follow Me Forward projects revealed powerful examples of authenticity in action.

One teacher tried a new protocol for her students while they worked independently. Students became so off task that she was unable to pull her small math groups without interruptions. It was, at first glance, a failure. However, she reflected on this and brainstormed alternatives to use in the coming days.

Another teacher realized they were not ready for visitors because student engagement was dropping. By reflecting, adjusting, and receiving honest feedback, the teacher was able to adjust and ultimately invite visitors into the classroom.

Finally, a principal honestly acknowledged they had not provided enough time for planning support and responded by committing to shifting the schedule to have uninterrupted time.

These moments are simple and ordinary and spark joy. These are the very things that should be at the heart of professional learning and evident in our schools.

Engagement and trust. In professional learning, authenticity fuels engagement and trust. When educators feel safe to be real about the things they know, what they don't, and what they're willing to try, learning becomes collaborative problem-solving, not an isolated performance review.

The Follow Me Forward Model structures this by creating regular spaces for teachers to polish and articulate their practice in low-stakes ways across all phases. This mirrors Brown's idea that authenticity is supported by clear expectations and norms, so participants can take risks without fear of humiliation.

Recent research supports this approach. For example, studies on psychological safety in peer mentoring (Laird et al., 2024) show that when educators trust the environment, they're more willing to engage in honest self-assessment, experiment with new strategies, and give and receive candid feedback. By weaving this into the Follow Me Forward Model for all participants, including leaders, everyone is able to rapidly increase capacity.

How Authenticity Guides Professional Learning

Because we value authenticity, it is not left to chance within the Follow Me Forward Model. We have purposefully built it into the design of each phase of the Learning Loops. From the outset, the Support Leaders model the vulnerability and authenticity they expect. Making it a practice to discuss what they are working on, what they find hard, and how they are learning from the hard parts and owning mistakes shows participants that not only do we say we value authenticity, we are aligning our actions with it.

In contrast, when evaluation is tied to punitive consequences and professional learning is really about compliance, being authentic can feel risky. There are several common barriers that can be addressed within the Follow Me Forward Model, so participants are free to be their true selves.

Common Barriers:

1. **Fear of judgement**
   Setting clear norms for each phase of the Learning Loops helps reduce a fear of being judged. There are discussion protocols, feedback guidelines, and clear indicators of successful practice, so participants stay focused on the bigger picture as well as work at the value level.

2. **Lack of time**
   Integrating authentic learning into the existing structures of school helps diminish the idea that professional learning is just one more thing to do. Providing clear times for debrief conversations and visitors helps participants feel honored and trusted as professionals. When this happens, they are able to show up authentically in those conversations.

3. **Resistance**
   By modeling authenticity, instructional leaders can set the tone for resistance. Celebration of small wins, using an asset based approach to feedback and showing how authenticity improves outcomes for students are all ways to reduce resistant behaviors.

Authenticity does not just appear in schools because we value it. It happens because we design for it.

Belonging

Professional Learning Today

Imagine walking into a cafeteria with rows of chairs set up, a PowerPoint flickering on the screen, and a presenter that reads the bullet points on slides. No one is invited to speak because the material must be covered in the allotted time. Questions are not allowed, or worse, they are pushed aside and ignored. The general consensus of participants is to just get through the event, so they can get to the things that matter. Belonging has no place here because the voices are silenced and energy is drained. This feels like exile, with no sense of community.

It is common for traditional approaches to professional learning to assume the participants know nothing about the topic at hand. This assumption does not take into account prior knowledge or unique experiences of the participants. It assumes, wrongly, that the presenter is all-knowing, and the others need to get up to speed. This is a perfect recipe for people to check out mentally and emotionally. The power structures in traditional professional learning create a sense of inadequacies and lack of belonging.

Alternatively, the Follow Me Forward Model creates the opposite. The value of belonging is one that is paramount and it is not an afterthought. Participants should feel a sense of belonging from the beginning and through the continuous learning loops. In fact, belonging is so important, we believe it is a high-leverage strategy to improve teacher performance and retention.

The What and Why of Belonging

In the Follow Me Forward Model, belonging is more than simply being accepted into a group. It is about being valued for who you are and knowing your voice matters. Fitting in, by contrast, is about adapting yourself to meet the expectations of others, often at the expense of your authentic self. In professional learning spaces, the difference matters deeply: when educators feel they belong, they bring their whole selves to the work, contributing honestly and innovating without fear. When they're just "fitting in," they often withhold ideas, avoid risk-taking, and default to compliance.

When we think about times that we truly belonged in professional settings, there were clear conditions that made that possible. The connections within the group and strength of the relationships led to an increase in engagement and willingness to share. For example, this can take the shape of a team meeting where all voices contribute to the conversation. It can also be a learning session where data is explored collaboratively, not just presented.

The sense of belonging in professional learning creates a foundation for trust, collaboration, and sustained growth. In the Follow Me Forward Model, belonging is intentionally cultivated through structures that encourage open dialogue, empower shared decision-making, and honor diverse expertise. This approach reduces the pressure to perform in a certain way and increases the willingness to engage in meaningful reflection and experimentation. Fitting in, on the other hand, can create a façade of harmony while masking disconnection and resistance.

When we link the value of belonging back to the work of William Powers, it fuels intrinsic motivation and builds professional resilience. These are two qualities essential for the kind of sustained change *Follow Me Forward* seeks to inspire and often result in more agency and self-efficacy on the part of the participants. Fitting in, on the other hand, may produce short-term compliance but rarely drives deep or lasting transformation.

How Belonging Guides Professional Learning

In the Follow Me Forward Model, we want educators to come as they are. This means no matter the years of experience or content expertise (or lack of), every educator has a place in this process.

In Phase 1 we encourage Support Leaders to meet people where they are. If the needs at the school call for classroom management support before we can address content, then no problem. If the sixth-grade team needs help with an inclusion model, perfect. If the math data indicate a need for more use of manipulatives, then we can help. The Follow Me Forward Model is one that can support all grades, all subjects, and almost all needs because the goals and success criteria are cocreated and based on real data needs. There is no need to create something else to do. By addressing gaps that are already there we set the stage for change.

It is worth noting here that supportive leaders play a particularly important role in the value of belonging. Early in the Follow Me Forward process, a Support Leader is selected to help bring people along the journey. When leaders take time to meet people where they are and design learning cultures to overcome barriers, not just create compliance, the generic work transforms into ways of being.

Transformational Learning

Jack Mezirow (1991) described transformational learning as a shift in perspective and how people see themselves in the world. For teachers, this might look like moving from compliance, (*I do this because the curriculum says so*) to agency (*I do this because it best serves my students*).

Transformation learning requires more than surface-level tips. It demands dialogue, questioning, and connections to core values. It happens when teachers examine not just their methods but how they see themselves as professionals. Transformation happens when educators are intentional about how they show up in classrooms.

The value work of *Follow Me Forward* helps teachers challenge their beliefs while continuing to have a guiding focus of lifelong learning, authenticity, and belonging. Learning occurs when people reflect, engage in dialogue, and lean into disorienting dilemmas that challenge prior beliefs.

When we think about the Being and Doing work built into the values, Mezirow's theory comes to life. If we want to be lifelong learners but consistently resist trying new things or just go through the motions in our classrooms, then we have to question how we are aligned as professionals. This Being/Doing alignment dissonance is often avoided in schools. We shy away from naming and discussing the deep-rooted disconnect in what we say we believe and what our actions show. In the Follow Me Forward Model, we welcome these dilemmas. We believe that in order for deep learning to take hold, we must emphasize a transformation of perspective.

This kind of change is not instant. It grows over time through authentic, sustained learning. It takes reflection and dialogue as we compare our actions to our values. In the Follow Me Forward Model, we build this time into each phase, so participants can transform not only *what* they do but—more importantly—*who* they become.

Summary

We want our students to think for themselves and make decisions. We want them to be able to self-regulate, create new thoughts, and become critical thinkers. We want them to think about their own thinking and grow as learners across their lifetime. We believe professional learning should do the same for educators.

The current professional development approaches fall short. They are often isolated events that are not created to transform the participants. Instead they are designed for following instructions, checking lists, and dutiful compliance. These models create conditions that stifle professional growth instead of cultivating it.

Creating a value-based professional learning system is needed now more than ever. Our values drive our beliefs, which in turn drive our actions. Addressing the whole educator within a professional learning model supports who we want to *be* in addition to what we want to *do.*

By weaving the values of lifelong learning, authenticity and belonging into one complete self-sustaining system, we embrace them as disciplined daily practices. They are supported by curious learning loops, collaborative conversations, and meaningful considerations for continual growth. The Follow Me Forward Model transforms professional learning from an event to an ongoing evolution of being.

Furthermore, the Follow Me Forward Model is designed not only for transformational change of teachers, but also school culture change. By creating conditions for teachers to be in positions of strength, they become change agents within the school as they move from blame to balance. It is this balance that ultimately transforms the culture into one where everyone thrives.

CHAPTER 2

Beliefs That Shape Lasting Learning

EARLY IN OUR CAREERS, WE participated in required training that resulted in little instructional improvement. One experience that stands out was a mandated after-school session required by our district related to integrated units. As teachers, we were told we needed to integrate our curriculum with other courses because that was the best practice. Unfortunately, our staff was not prepared for this kind of work. There were divisions that ran deep across grade levels and subject areas. There were huge gaps in experiences, backgrounds, and expectations for effective instruction. Some groups worked in the proverbial silos, and others were just surviving the day. Looking back, we simply did not get along and had very different values about teaching and learning.

In this particular session, the presenter tasked us with working in small groups to identify ways our curriculum overlapped. It went poorly. Some people did not have the understanding of the courses the way others did, some people had preconceived notions about the people in their group, and some of them just did not want to change what they had always done. In response to the dysfunction of the groups, the presenter tried to tell everyone to put differences aside, complete the task, and move on. Instead of solving the problem, the presenter offended some faculty who did not feel seen and heard, and those teachers walked out of the session. Ignoring the roots of the dysfunction escalated tensions and ultimately ended the session.

As a young teacher, Alice had no idea what to think or how to react. Was this something that happened all the time, and if so why would anyone want to come to required workshops or sessions? It felt odd to be in education and hate learning. It seemed counterproductive because it was. The issues of this session ran so deep there was no way a one-hour session was going to create real change. Ironically it united enemies (if only briefly) against the instructor.

Professional learning is supposed to be the engine that drives teacher growth, instructional improvement, and ultimately student achievement. However, most teachers describe their experiences with what is referred to as professional development as falling short of any sort of growth.

The Problem with Traditional Professional Learning

Many educators report feeling like professional initiatives are things that are done *to* them instead of done *with* them. One veteran teacher told us, "It seems like every August we sit in the media center for hours. They roll out the big binder or the latest initiative, and by September, it's collecting dust on my shelf. None of it really connects to the students in front of me."

This frustration stems from familiar professional development pitfalls:

Professional development is a one-time event. People assemble, get the information, and leave. There is an absence of ongoing support. There is little follow-up, coaching, or sustained reflection. The content does not align with other initiatives or student needs. Teachers return to their classrooms only to become overwhelmed and abandon the work.

Professional development is isolating. There is a lack of collaboration. Participants are passive, leaders are absent, and the scalability is low. Teachers often teach their own version and may be reluctant to share ideas or collaborate.

Professional development is generic. One-size-fits-all delivery is commonplace. A visiting international teacher and a twenty-year veteran teacher sit side-by-side in the same training. Both leave with different understandings and applications. Sessions are often oriented around content but not a relevant problem to solve. Meaning is missing.

The result? Teachers describe these experiences as compliance-based, irrelevant, and exhausting. It becomes something to sit through rather than something that fuels growth. It is seen as the thing they must do before they get to the things that matter.

At its worst, bad professional learning sessions can erode morale. When teachers feel their time is wasted, it sends a message: "Your challenges don't matter. We don't see you." That breeds cynicism, which is the last thing we want if we aim to empower our teachers. Alice perceived professional development as another way to highlight divisions and issues with capacity instead of bringing groups together.

Despite all of this, we believe that teachers want to grow. It has been our experience teachers are hungry for learning that makes a difference. What they need is adult learning that lasts.

A Different Way Forward

Imagine a process where curiosity drives the questions and dialogue that lead to exploration of new practices. Envision a professional learning model where teachers look forward to gathering together. Think about a place where the experience feels meaningful, not compliant, and each person's voice matters in shaping the work. Time feels well spent because it is connected directly to students and the challenges teachers care about most. This is a meaningful space that honors curiosity and collaboration.

This vision of professional learning isn't just better. It's a different model entirely, not only value-based, but also grounded in research about how adults learn.

Professional Learning Comparison Chart

Curiosity

Feature	Traditional Workshops	Instructional Coaching	Follow Me Forward Model
Delivery Format	• One-time presenter-led sessions • Little inquiry	• One-on-one or small group • Coach as leader	• Hybrid model with learning loops, coaching, leadership, and immersion • Designed to spark questions and exploration
Sustainability	• Low • Curiosity is not cultivated before or beyond the session	• Medium • Depends on teacher-coach relationship	• High • Structures sustain ongoing inquiry and teacher-driven discovery

Feature	Traditional Workshops	Instructional Coaching	Follow Me Forward Model
Data Use	• None or limited • May use exit slips • No follow-ups	• Varies • Shaped by coach priorities	• Ongoing • Uses formative assessment tools • Pursuit of understanding student thinking
Focus	• Attendance/Compliance	• Growth of individual teacher skills	• Systemic transformation • Curiosity fuels problem-solving and continuous improvement

Collaboration

Feature	Traditional Workshops	Instructional Coaching	Follow Me Forward Model
Teacher Role	• Passive recipient	• Active participant	• Cocreator of learning and change through learning loops
Leader Involvement	• Minimal to none	• Occasional observation or support	• Embedded leadership development
Scalability	• Limited • Not easily repeatable	• Varies • Limited by coaching capacity	• Strong • Designed for schoolwide adoption

Feature	Traditional Workshops	Instructional Coaching	Follow Me Forward Model
Resources Provided	• Handouts or slides only	• Coach-developed tools	• Resources developed as needed

Meaning

Feature	Traditional Workshops	Instructional Coaching	Follow Me Forward Model
Connection to Daily Practice	• Low • Often theoretical	• Medium • Varies by coach	• High • Experiential, job-embedded learning • Aligned to authentic work
Customization	• One-size-fits-all	• Personalized but inconsistent	• Customized to meet participant capacity
Alignment to School Improvement Plan	• Often based on trends or politics	• Sometimes aligned	• Directly mapped to cocreated goals and continuum of practice

Adult Learning Principles

Malcolm Knowles (1984) changed the conversation about adult learning when he introduced the idea of *andragogy*. Andragogy is the practice of teaching adult learners. Knowles argued that adults learn differently from children because they bring lived experiences, self-direction, and practical needs into every learning environment.

Knowles' principles can be summarized like this:

- Adults are self-directed learners.
- They bring prior experiences that shape new learning.
- They are motivated when learning is relevant to real-life tasks.
- They prefer problem-centered approaches to abstract content.

When applied to professional learning, these ideas challenge the very fibers of "sit-and-get" training. If teachers are to learn as adults, they must have ownership. They must see the connection to their work. They must be treated as professionals, not passive recipients who are blank slates.

In addition, research shows that curiosity, collaboration, and meaning are powerful drivers of adult learning. When adults are able to explore questions that spark curiosity, engage with colleagues in authentic collaboration, and connect learning to meaningful purposes, they are more motivated. This also leads to more sustainability over time (Deci & Ryan, 2000; Knowles, Holton, Swanson, 2015). In our work, we have seen this play out over and over again. The kind of professional learning that lights up teachers is the kind that solves a real problem they are having instead of delivering content to kick off a new school year. Because of this, these beliefs are a critical aspect of the Follow Me Forward Model.

In one of our sessions, we were presenting best practices for making thinking visible. One of the participants had some experience with this but noticed her students continued to specifically struggle with making inferences, which is an important comprehension strategy for successful readers. Instead of telling her that was not the focus of our work, we dug into this idea. We helped her learn more about the thinking processes involved with making inferences and consider ways for her to teach her students these ideas. The result was a curious teacher who went back to her classroom equipped with a meaningful, concrete next step to try with her students. This is powerful adult learning.

The Three Beliefs of Lasting Learning

The values we hold drive our beliefs, and our beliefs ultimately drive our actions. Building on the firm foundations of values from Chapter 1, we have combined the adult learning research with three specific beliefs that enable transformational change:

1. **We believe curiosity fuels deep learning.**
2. **We believe collaboration is key because learning is social.**
3. **We believe meaningful work is the key to sustainability.**

Together, these beliefs create a system where learning becomes part of the professional culture, not just an event. It fosters habits of becoming, not compliance.

BELIEF ONE:
Curiosity fuels deep learning

Learning that lasts is not a single event. It's a cycle that includes a process of trying, reflecting, and trying again in response to what we notice. For teachers, growth happens in the same way it does for students: through repetition, practice, and responsiveness. A one-day workshop might spark interest, but without opportunities to revisit and deepen the learning, the sparks fizzle out quickly. True change opportunities can be missed. Curiosity fuels inquiry and reflection that leads to new insights.

In Follow Me Forward schools, curiosity takes on many forms:

- **Learning sparks curiosity across the full year.** Instead of frontloading all the learning into beginning-of-the-year workshop days, momentum is sustained by inviting teachers back into continuous Learning Loops. Teachers ask new questions as their classrooms evolve. Ongoing sessions are seen as opportunities to wonder and revisit ideas we discover together.
- **Feedback fuels curiosity over time.** Support sessions and informal conversations become vessels for feedback. Like athletes working with a coach, teachers need someone who can observe, offer targeted feedback, and help them consider, "What if?" Professional growth becomes less about evaluation and more about curiosity driving improvement over time. Feedback becomes a gift.
- **Structures encourage curiosity in growth.** Professional growth should not feel like a checklist but an evolutionary journey. Regular conversations around indicators of practice give teachers space to reflect and ask questions then set fresh goals on what they notice. In this way, curiosity becomes the spark that keeps motivation alive.

Curiosity connects directly to the Follow Me Forward value of lifelong learning. It tells teachers, "We want to know what interests you, and we'll walk beside you as you learn." This is a powerful cultural message. Instead of sending the signal that professional learning is just another series of random, disconnected information-sharing sessions, schools communicate that growth is personalized, ongoing, and supported.

Curiosity is also an important role with administrators. Rather than being organizers of isolated professional learning events, leaders become architects of learning cultures. They design routines where feedback, collaboration, and practice are woven into the school's daily fabric because they remain curious. They value this work and honor the time and energy it takes. When teachers see that their learning and curiosity matter consistently, not just every now and then, the culture of growth becomes contagious.

Follow Me Forward Story

One of the teachers who participated in the Follow Me Forward Model was struggling with teacher talk. Ms. Salinas self-reported not being able to fit everything she wanted in her instructional block. She struggled to review homework, clarify misconceptions, complete the whole-class lesson, and pull her small groups. After collecting classroom data, Ms. Salinas and Alice discussed the amount of time she was talking as opposed to the students working. By tracking the time across several lessons, they identified places in the instructional block where she could focus on trimming her teacher talk, thus increasing time for student work.

By intentionally gathering information (data), reflecting, and collaboratively goal-setting, Ms. Salinas decided to set a timer to help raise her awareness and keep herself on track, so she could release students to work more quickly. With this simple change, Ms. Salinas was able to increase students' time on task and increase her sense of agency about being a lifelong learner. Success breeds success. By the end of our work together, she reported an increase in self efficacy and a transformation as a professional.

BELIEF TWO:
Collaboration is key because learning is social

If curiosity drives growth, collaboration is one way to strengthen it and keep it alive. It is difficult to carry the weight of professional growth alone. When teachers collaborate, they exchange ideas, challenge assumptions, and encourage one another to try new approaches. We believe learning is social, and therefore, the best learning happens in community. Our work is human to human.

In Follow Me Forward schools, collaboration looks like this:

- **With collaboration, meetings matter.** When meetings move beyond filling out meeting minutes and instead dig deeply into student work, they become powerful engines of change. Teachers analyze evidence, ask probing questions, and plan responsive instruction together. This is more than an exercise in compliance.

- **With collaboration, peer observations foster growth, not judgment.** Creating a culture where teachers regularly open their doors, not to be evaluated but to learn from one another, is valuable. A fifth-grade teacher can pick up a new questioning strategy from a colleague in science, or a high school biology teacher can learn about grouping techniques from an English teacher. This is the opposite of competitive work; it becomes collegial.
- **With collaboration, there is rich cross-disciplinary dialogue.** Instead of working in silos, teachers can collaborate horizontally and vertically. When teachers from different content areas or grade levels share practices, surprising innovations occur. A literacy strategy used in English class might unlock deeper comprehension in social studies class.

When teachers feel seen, heard, and supported by colleagues, their professional load feels lighter. This belief in collaboration links directly back to the Follow Me Forward value of belonging because teaching can be isolating. A teacher can spend an entire day in a room with students without ever having a meaningful conversation with another adult. They can fall into tunnel vision, lack perspective to see what to do next, and overlook what is working well. Professional collaboration interrupts that isolation and reminds teachers that they are part of something larger. It is more important than ever for teachers to believe and feel they are not alone in the work they do. We learn better when we learn together.

Follow Me Forward Story

As a participant in one of our Follow Me Forward schools, Mr. Hinkle was hesitant to believe any of the changes he made would matter. He was a veteran teacher, had been around the block a few times, and "only had a few years" before retirement. When Mr. Hinkle was able to visit a colleague's classroom and have a conversation with her about her instructional decisions, he changed. He noticed some simple procedures she had in place that directly addressed some engagement problems he was trying to solve. The very problems he thought were unsolvable were not issues in the room he observed. By talking with her about her processes and procedures, he was able to figure out his own next steps. He went back to his classroom and implemented new routines immediately. The collaborative nature of this work is how he was able to make change so quickly.

BELIEF THREE:
Meaningful work is the key to sustainability

One of the biggest issues in professional learning is how to sustain the initiatives. In *Follow Me Forward*, we believe meaning is the key. If professional learning isn't something useful, teachers will tune it out. Meaningful work means every session, conversation, and resource must connect directly to the realities of teaching. It is intentional and purposeful. When learning connects to purpose, it lasts.

With limited time and countless demands, teachers naturally ask, "How will this help me tomorrow?" If the answer is unclear, attention drifts, and motivation plummets. But if professional learning connects directly to their classroom and student needs, engagement skyrockets.

In Follow Me Forward schools, meaningful work looks like this:

- **Meaningful professional learning is rooted in formative data.** Teachers should leave sessions with strategies they can apply immediately to the very challenges their students face. For example, if formative assessments reveal reading comprehension gaps, the professional learning should target those gaps with practical, usable tools.

- **Meaningful professional learning is differentiated.** Just as students need differentiation, so do teachers. One size rarely fits all. A novice teacher might need classroom management basics, while a veteran teacher seeks advanced strategies for instructional leadership. Meaningful work means meeting teachers where they are with professional practice and considering what they bring to the experience within a continuum.

- **Meaningful professional learning is timely and responsive.** Meaningful work requires agility. If a school is experiencing behavioral challenges, waiting until next year's professional learning plan is too late. Meaningful professional learning addresses urgent issues in real time.

These beliefs around meaning connect to the *Follow Me Forward* value of authenticity. Teachers are quick to spot when something is fabricated. But when professional learning is real, the engagement increases. Teachers are motivated when their work connects to the larger mission of helping students thrive and helps them become the professional they want to be. Meaning drives lifelong learning because it reminds educators that we really are never done. Our growth is never finished because new insights open doors for more learning. Meaning also reinforces authenticity, allowing for teachers to act in alignment rather than just following mandates. Belonging is increased when teachers recognize their roles in a shared, meaningful mission.

Follow Me Forward Story

At West End Middle School, there was a scheduled teacher workday in the fall semester. Instead of pulling everyone together in the media center and conducting a workshop, the principal chose to conduct multiple mini-sessions throughout the morning, so teachers could attend several sessions of interest. One of the sessions was built around the Follow Me Forward Model in progress on that campus. The ERG consultant suggested a panel discussion instead of a traditional workshop as a way to inform the nonparticipants in the school about the work.

When the day came, Ms. Salinas and Mrs. Morrigan shared how they got started, what lessons they had learned, how it was going, etc. as the ERG consultant moderated. Instead of sitting through a workshop, teachers were able to hear directly from their colleagues, ask real questions, and consider ways to start in their own rooms.

Seeing and hearing from colleagues as they discussed data on their own students, talked about ways to differentiate teaching styles, and consider the alignment with their own school goals was powerful. Participants were engaged, and their exit ticket responses shared how much they enjoyed the session format compared to a traditional workshop. In addition, several teachers approached the principal and asked how they could be a part of the next learning loop.

Kolb's Experiential Learning Cycle & Learning Loops

The Follow Me Forward Learning Loops are intentionally designed for experiential learning. David Kolb's Experiential Learning Theory (1984) argued that learning is not linear. Instead, he suggested learning is cyclical, moving through distinct stages:

1. **Concrete Experience:** Trying something new.
2. **Reflective Observation:** Reflecting on and analyzing what happened.
3. **Abstract Conceptualization:** Forming new ideas and drawing conclusions based on reflections (Being)
4. **Active Experimentation:** Applying the new concepts (Doing)

In traditional professional development approaches, teachers are often given only abstract concepts such as strategies or theories without time for real experiences, reflection, or experimentation. That's like telling people how to swim without ever getting into the water. It sounds great and is fast, but it is not very effective and definitely not sustainable.

The Follow Me Forward Model honors Kolb's full learning cycle.

In the Follow Me Forward Model, educators journey together through five interconnected phases of growth known as *learning loops*. Each loop represents a continuous cycle of professional learning. This is an embodiment of lifelong learning, authenticity, and belonging. Rather than treating professional development as a "one and done," learning loops invite participants into an ongoing, collaborative process where reflection, renewal, and shared purpose sustain momentum.

The first learning loop begins with a small group of teachers who value curiosity, collaboration, and meaning as the drivers of their professional growth. Teachers try new strategies in their classrooms, reflect with colleagues, extract lessons learned, and test new approaches again across the phases. This dynamic process results in high engagement and rapid building of capacity. These participants then engage in a second loop that builds upon the first.

As new participants join, additional loops form, overlapping and spiraling upward across school years. This growing spiral symbolizes the living culture of *Follow Me Forward*: professional learning that is continuous, authentic, and woven into the fabric of the school community.

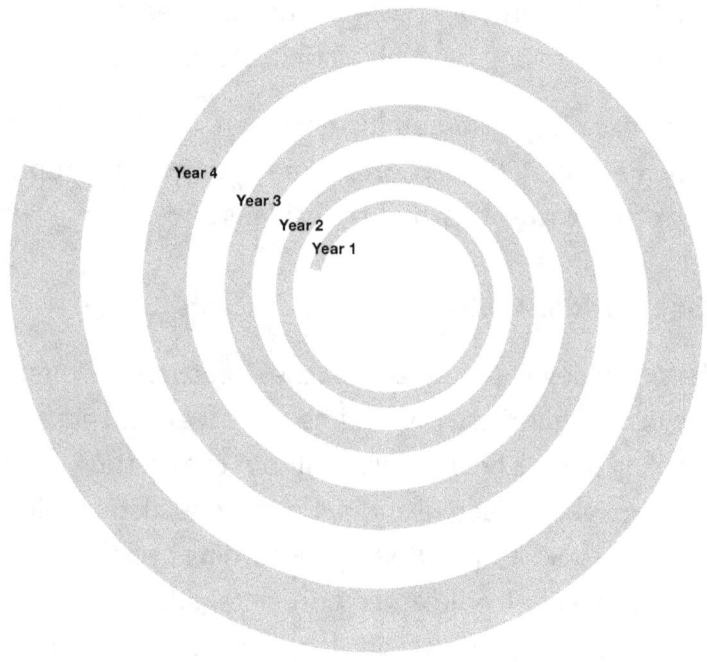

Summary

Teachers today are under enormous pressure. They juggle curriculum demands, diverse student needs, and the weight of public expectations. They don't need more binders or workshops. They need learning that is meaningful and honors who they are as adult professionals.

The difference between traditional professional development and *Follow Me Forward* can be summed up in three shifts:

- Moving from training events → to curious learning cycles.
- Moving from isolation → to collaboration.
- Moving from generic work → to meaningful considerations.

This is not a program. *Follow Me Forward* is a new way of seeing and experiencing professional learning. It is holistic, value-driven, and aligned with how adults are motivated to learn. For principals and administrators, the call is clear: adopting *Follow Me Forward* is not about chasing trends. It's about designing a model where teacher growth is sustained, authentic, and connected to student outcomes.

We know professional learning should move beyond one-time events and instead unfold as curious learning loops that evolve with the needs of educators and their classrooms. Collaboration is key to a sustainable professional development system where shared actions, routines, and problem-solving connect us as a professional community. Meaningful work grounds us at the relationship level so every strategy, resource, and conversation directly connects to the real needs of teachers, students and larger school communities. It gives us purpose. Combined, these beliefs uphold our highest values and turn them into purposeful action by keeping professional learning focused, practical, and deeply connected to the whole educator.

By grounding professional learning in andragogy, building on the beliefs and designing learning loops that include the values of lifelong learning, authenticity, and belonging, we have created a system that fuels both teacher motivation and student success. It is holistic and human to human. Because humans are at the heart of professional learning.

PART 2

Collaborative Learning Loops

CHAPTER 3

Phase 1:
Create a Culture for Host Teachers

Overview of Phase 1

1. Select a Support Leader
2. Check In – Values and Beliefs
3. Identify Host Teachers
4. Gather Data
5. Set Goals
6. Develop a Continuum of Practice

Step 1: Select a Support Leader

The entire administration team should be aligned with the values and beliefs of *Follow Me Forward*. However, one individual must be identified as the Support Leader. This leader becomes the guiding light who walks alongside Host Teachers in a learning loop, coordinates the process, and ensures fidelity to the model.

Step 2: Check In – Values and Beliefs

The *Making the Shift: Beliefs About Professional Learning* inventory serves as an anchor for the model. By completing it, teachers and administrators surface their current beliefs about professional learning and reflect on their own readiness for growth. This process provides the administration team and Support Leader with authentic insight into beliefs, perspectives, and potential, while giving teachers the space to engage in meaningful self-reflection.

Step 3: Identify Host Teachers

The administration team including the Support Leader extends personal invitations to two to four Host Teachers. These Host Teachers commit to a year-long journey in which they will do the following:

- Participate in targeted training.
- Observe a demonstration lesson.
- Engage in three structured support sessions designed to provide high-level, growth-oriented feedback.
- Open their classrooms to colleagues for collaborative learning.

Step 4: Gather Data

Host Teachers and the Support Leader analyze holistic data in order to go beyond test scores. Observations, teacher notes, and samples of student work all provide valuable evidence of student thinking and are used to guide goal-setting.

Step 5: Set Goals

After reviewing data, clear goals are established. These goals are rooted in real classroom needs rather than mandates, ensuring that learning is both relevant and student-centered.

Step 6: Develop a Continuum of Practice

Once goals are set, the Host Teacher and Support Leader codevelop a Continuum of Practice with three stages: Foundation, Expansion, and Refinement. This guiding document serves as a roadmap, making progress visible and manageable, and supporting self-assessment and growth along the way.

Step 1: Select a Support Leader

The Follow Me Forward Model for lasting change unfolds through collaborative learning loops across five phases over one school year, starting with the all-important Phase 1. Think of this as a path where a collaborative group walks together. The collaborative group has selected to be on the path, they belong on the path and are all becoming the next version of themselves as educators as they walk on the path forward.

On this path, there *must* be a Support Leader to light the way. That Support Leader may be a principal, an assistant principal, an instructional facilitator, a school coach, an ERG consultant, or a teacher at the school who has read this book and wants to step out and lead and light the way through the professional learning journey. Titles matter less than the commitment to guide, encourage, and sustain momentum on the path forward. What matters most is that a Support Leader is deeply committed to value-based and belief-based professional learning.

The following statements can help identify the right person to light the path as a Support Leader:

- I value **lifelong learning** and believe teachers in my school can grow **curiosity** about the best ways to facilitate learning in their classrooms.
- I value **authenticity** and believe learning is about **meaning** and relevance—not about perfection, but a collaborative process of practice, self-reflection, and polish with feedback.
- I value **belonging** and believe it is possible to build a culture of **collaboration** where teachers feel connected and supported beyond their classrooms.

Individuals who align with these values and beliefs are potential Support Leaders. The administration team at the school obviously has an important place in reinforcing the Support Leader. All stakeholders should be aligned with values and beliefs that underpin the Follow Me Forward Model. Schools may choose to hire ERG support. When schools bring in ERG support, they benefit from the expertise and prior experience with the Follow Me Forward Model, but also from a collaborative coaching partnership. In these cases, the ERG consultant works alongside the Support Leader, coaching shoulder to shoulder, while intentionally building the leadership capacity of the Support Leader along the way. See Follow Me Forward Roles (Appendix 1).

Step 2: Check In – Values and Beliefs

After a Support Leader has been identified, the next step in Phase 1 is to invite teachers to respond to the Follow Me Forward values and belief inventory: *Making the Shift: Values and Beliefs About Professional Learning*. This important anchor tool uses a Likert scale to capture how teachers and administrators currently view professional learning and how the values of lifelong learning, authenticity, and belonging, and the beliefs of curiosity, collaboration, and meaning fit into their current professional landscape. It is important to contextualize the inventory rather than present it as a stand-alone task. Teachers are introduced to the idea of becoming a Follow Me Forward School by learning about the five phases that guide the process. In doing so, teachers understand that the inventory is not just a diagnostic task, but a reflective opportunity that allows them to consider their values, beliefs, and readiness for growth within a larger, collaborative vision of change taking place at their school.

> **Bonus Resources:** For a downloadable copy of *Making the Shift: Values and Beliefs About Professional Learning*, please visit www.myedresource.com.

Who will participate in the first learning loop? There are options.

- **Option 1** – All teachers in the school can respond to the inventory. This can enable a schoolwide conversation about professional learning values and beliefs and becoming a Follow Me Forward School.
- **Option 2** – A grade level can respond to the inventory. This can enable a critical mass at the school to begin a conversation about professional learning values and beliefs and becoming a Follow Me Forward School.
- **Option 3** – There can be a call for volunteers to begin a conversation about professional learning values and beliefs and becoming a Follow me Forward School. These volunteers respond to the inventory.

In a culture of continuous improvement, the beliefs educators hold about professional learning profoundly shape how they engage with the school culture and the values they find important. The insights gained from the *Making the Shift* inventory guide everyone involved in the process. Teachers check in with their beliefs related to professional learning, while the administration team and the Support Leader reflects on readiness, building trust, and honoring the teacher's voice from the very beginning.

This is not just an exercise; it is the foundation of a collaborative path toward lasting change. It marks the start of a journey in which teachers define who they want to be as educators, what they believe about instruction and student learning, and what they value as educators. This is the beginning of building a culture where teachers feel a sense of belonging. For this reason, we cannot overstate the importance of taking the time to invite teachers to respond to the inventory as a first step, reflect on the results, and begin meaningful conversations. Without this intentional beginning, the Follow Me Forward Model risks feeling like "just one more thing" added to teachers' already full load.

Step 3: Identify Host Teachers

Information about values and beliefs related to professional learning from the *Making the Shift* inventory have been gathered and debrief conversations have taken place. With this foundation in place, it is time to officially invite Host Teachers who will walk the path and make a learning loop across five phases of the Follow Me Forward Model, over one school year, with the Support Leader.

One of the most powerful aspects of the Follow Me Forward Model is that it places teachers, not programs, at the center of professional growth. At the heart of this approach are Host Teachers: educators who are willing to open their classrooms to their colleagues as living laboratories where learning is visible, energizing, and collaborative. But Host Teachers are not chosen at random, nor are they simply the "best" or most seasoned.

The administration team, along with the Support Leader, extend an invitation to teachers who have shown that they value lifelong learning, authenticity, and belonging and believe in curiosity, collaboration, and meaning. The invitation to become a Host Teacher should be personal and purposeful. It's not an announcement of a mandate in a staff meeting or a call for volunteers in an email. It can be a one-on-one conversation that says,

> "We are working as a school to embed professional learning in real classrooms where teachers learn from each other through the Follow Me Forward Model. Would you be willing to be a host classroom teacher? As a Host Teacher you will have exclusive training, receive support sessions with feedback, and grow as a leader by opening your classroom to peers for collaborative learning."

Potential Host Teachers should understand that they are being invited not because they're outstanding or they need help, but because they exemplify the values and beliefs of the Follow Me Forward Model.

What makes this role of Host Teacher so attractive is that it's a chance for the Host Teacher to grow as well as help others all while doing their day-to-day work of teaching. The invitation should explain that as part of the Follow Me Forward Model, Host Teachers receive high-level support from a Support Leader who is embedded in the school or a consultant, such as Education Resource Group, brought into the school to support the learning journey. They are supported through all phases of the model, have time and space to reflect, and are provided with strength-based feedback. They gain leadership experience and develop skills they will carry with them throughout their careers and as they continuously build their belief system and what they value as a teacher.

Perhaps most importantly, they are reminded that their classroom can be a place where change begins—not with perfect lessons, but with honest conversations, shared learning with colleagues, and a sense of belonging. This model normalizes the idea that growth happens through a process of trying, adjusting, and trying again. This mirrors the authentic ways we learn in our real lives when learning something new. It fosters a culture where teachers don't feel like they're on stage, but instead feel like they're part of a learning community. They are able to figure things out together as their colleagues visit their classrooms and reflect on the visit.

In the first year, invitations are extended to two to four teachers to become Host Teachers. Don't mistake the small number of teachers involved as "starting small." These few classrooms create a ripple effect. As colleagues visit the Host Teacher's classroom, they begin to see what's possible. A culture of collaboration begins to take root in the school. And before long, the shift moves beyond classrooms; it starts to shape the identity of the school.

Recruiting Host Teachers should never be about compliance or punishment. It is about invitation and inspiration.

Step 4: Gather Data

Rather than prescribing a top-down initiative based solely on test scores, the Follow Me Forward Model centers the voices of teachers in identifying instructional goals. This is where holistic data becomes essential. Instead of looking only at test scores, Support Leaders and Host Teachers reflect on rich, classroom-based insight from one or multiple sources listed below:

- Observations of student engagement and participation

- Analysis of student work
- Anecdotal notes
- Student beliefs about learning
- Performance tasks
- Student portfolios
- Student interviews or inventories
- Formative assessments
- School improvement plans
- Test scores

This holistic lens ensures that professional learning is grounded in classroom realities, rather than only external mandates and test scores.

Follow Me Forward Story

Over the past several years, Alice has worked as the Support Leader at several middle schools. At one middle school, two seventh-grade ELA teachers expressed concern about low student engagement and participation during whole-group instruction. They decided to observe each other to collect data related to their concerns. When they observed each other, they used their rosters to tally observable behaviors (e.g., raised hand, answering, contributing to discussion, eye contact, on task behavior.) This observational data became the catalyst to consider new ways of reaching students during the ELA time.

Step 5: Set Goals

Once data has been reviewed, it is used to set goals and develop a plan for implementation. Historically, teachers have been given mandates and curriculum to be taught and in some situations scripts. In this case, allowing teachers to have voice in setting goals may be difficult for them. If this is the case, Support Leaders will need to guide teachers on how to use holistic data and have a voice with setting instructional goals and developing stages of implementation.

> **Follow Me Forward Story**
>
> *After observing each other and collecting data, our ELA teachers took time to reflect on their data and consider goals to better reach their students in ELA time. They expressed their concerns with their principal and Alice, and from there came up with the following goals:*
>
> - *Make a shift toward teaching more often in small groups—reducing whole-group instruction.*
> - *Increase opportunities for productive small-group learning in ELA.*
>
> *Together, Alice, the principal, and the teachers clarified the goals and discussed a format for small-group instruction. They agreed on a structure where the majority of students would work independently on meaningful tasks while the teacher strategically met with small groups for approximately 20 minutes each at the teacher table. Each group was formed around common needs, allowing instruction to be focused and responsive.*

Step 6: Develop a Continuum of Practice

Once the goals are set, a Continuum of Practice is developed by the Support Leader and Host Teachers. This document captures three stages (Foundation, Expansion, and Refinement) and serves as a roadmap, making the indicators visible and manageable. By progressing stage-by-stage, Host Teachers are able to see the progression of implementation, self-assess along the way, and celebrate growth. These three stages are especially helpful for Host Teachers who want perfection immediately. Host Teachers do not all have to move through these three stages at the same pace and in the same way.

Foundation Stage

At the Foundation Stage, the work is just beginning. Teachers and students are exploring new processes and building foundational skills. Success is not yet consistent, but the groundwork is being laid. Teachers model frequently, provide support and help students build stamina and confidence. This stage matters because it is where small deliberate steps begin to form lasting habits.

Expansion Stage

At the Expansion Stage, consistency starts to take shape. Teachers begin releasing more responsibility to students as routines run more smoothly and confidence grows. Instruction is informed by data, and students start showing ownership in their learning. This stage is about practice. Host Teachers try new strategies, notice what works, and make thoughtful adjustments. Growth here is reflected in moving from "sometimes" to "more often" in both student actions and teacher decisions.

Refinement Stage

At the Refinement Stage, practices are intentional and responsive. Teachers make flexible, data-driven choices and offer feedback that propels learning forward. Instruction feels seamless because the teacher and student actions align naturally with the learning goal. This stage represents a polished, sustainable level of practice where consistency leads to automaticity and confidence.

In short:
- The **Foundation Stage** marks the *starting point*.
- The **Expansion Stage** captures the *process of growth*.
- The **Refinement Stage** illustrates what *strong, consistent, and sustainable practice* looks like.

Together, they form a clear pathway for progress that honors authentic learning as a journey.

Follow Me Forward Story

Below is an example of the Continuum of Practice Alice developed with the teachers mentioned above - ELA teachers with goals: 1. Make a shift toward teaching more often in small groups—reducing whole-group instruction and 2.Increase opportunities for productive small-group learning in ELA.

Continuum of Practice

Goals:

1. *Make a shift toward teaching more often in small groups—reducing whole-group instruction.*
2. *Increase opportunities for productive small-group learning in ELA.*

Foundation Stage	
Student Indicators	• Students can sometimes sustain independent work on meaningful, manageable tasks. • Students begin to problem-solve issues with some success.
Teacher Indicators	• The teacher establishes and demonstrates clear processes and procedures. • The teacher clarifies expectations for independent time. • The teacher models routines and provides guidance and feedback as students build stamina.
Notes and Reflections	

Expansion Stage	
Student Indicators	• Students sustain independent work for a minimum of 20 minutes. • Students transition smoothly through rotations. • Students use materials and resources productively. • Students problem-solve issues independently of the teacher.
Teacher Indicators	(for small groups) • The teacher forms small groups based on relevant data. • The teacher sets a clear, standards-aligned purpose for lessons. • The teacher provides targeted feedback related to the purpose. • The teacher notices and records student thinking. • The teacher begins analyzing notes to consider next steps. • The teacher usually releases most of the time to students for learning while observing their thinking.
Notes and Reflections	

Refinement Stage *Includes all indicators from the Foundation and Expansion stages, plus the following*	
Student Indicators	• Students demonstrate consistent high engagement and quality output. • Students use a wide variety of texts (fiction, nonfiction, poetry, articles, etc.). • Student-to-student dialogue increases. • Students regularly reflect and set personal goals.
Teacher Indicators	• The teacher consistently uses multiple data sources to plan and flex groups (not only at assessment times). • The teacher maintains a systematic record-keeping process for notes. • The teacher articulates patterns from student thinking to plan next steps. • The teacher models teacher thinking transparently. • The teacher gives effective feedback to students that moves learning forward. • The teacher facilitates high-level, purposeful conversations aligned with standards and academic vocabulary. • The teacher responsively adjusts instruction based on what is learned during the lesson.
Notes and Reflections	

Lesson Snapshot & Goals

Elementary Case Study: Franklin Elementary School

At Franklin Elementary school, a routine second-grade team meeting evolved into a powerful moment of reflection. Teachers openly acknowledged the wide range of student needs in math and expressed growing concern about how to address them effectively. Many students, they noted, demonstrated only a surface-level grasp of mathematical concepts, struggling to engage in deeper, conceptual thinking.

Recognizing this as an organic opportunity to support authentic growth, the principal reached out to her supervisor for guidance. Together, they called ERG to explore the Follow Me Forward Model and were immediately drawn to its values of lifelong learning, authenticity, and belonging.

Inspired by the model's potential, the principal invited her second-grade team to reflect on their current instructional practices and consider their readiness for change.

To deepen this reflection, she introduced the *Making the Shift: Values and Beliefs About Professional Learning* inventory, prompting teachers to consider their level of readiness. In addition, she outlined the benefits of being a Host Teacher and the five phases to help teachers see how this work could unfold over time.

Because the conversation had started organically in a grade-level meeting with all six second-grade teachers, the principal extended an invitation to all six second-grade teachers to consider starting a learning loop as Host Teachers. In this key structure, colleagues engage in classroom visits to observe each other and learn in real time.

The result: Three of the six second-grade teachers volunteered to become Host Teachers. This moment marked the beginning of authentic change anchored in teacher voice, collaborative reflection, and a shared commitment to instructional improvement through the FMF model.

The three teachers and the principal decided to explore small-group math instruction and teachers had a big part in setting goals for the initiative. With guidance from their ERG Support Leader, they set the following goals:

1. Use the data available to identify students who had foundational issues with the math standard they were teaching, students who were ready to learn the math standard they were teaching, and students who already knew the math standard they were teaching.
2. Agree on a format for the small-group math lesson.
3. Decide what the students away from the teacher table would be doing.

Middle School Case Study: West End Middle School

The principal of West End Middle School noticed that there was a consistent plateau of achievement for certain groups of students in the building. Over the years, it had become typical for the math scores to remain flat (or even decline) despite efforts to stop it. Noticing the need for change, this principal started a conversation with one of her most seasoned math teachers who in turn, took a deeper dive into the student results data from the end of year achievement tests.

What she found was interesting. Her overall data was fine. There was nothing alarming in the proficiency results, but when she segmented the data differently, she realized her students who were identified as academically and intellectually gifted (AIG) were not getting expected results. In fact, these students scored proficiently but showed a decline in growth data. This means they started the year with a projected score determined by state algorithms, and they did not meet it while still operating above grade level. This was causing a dip in the overall growth data for the grade level and the school.

Meanwhile, in another classroom, a teacher was also exploring the concept of achievement growth amongst her students. When she dug into her individual student scores, she found the same thing. The AIG students were not growing at the rate the algorithm predicted despite showing up as proficient as individuals, for the grade and the school.

The principal selected ERG as the Support Leader at the school level. She discussed what she was seeing with ERG and wanted the professional learning to organically form around the voices of teachers. When ERG first met with the teachers, there was a check-in on values, beliefs, and specific goals they wanted to achieve and general thoughts about professional learning.

Because both of these teachers bravely voiced their concerns and wondered what was going on with the AIG groups, the principal supported this work in a radical way. She invited only these teachers to have support. By not mandating but instead offering an invitation to work in a different way, this principal set the stage for transformational learning. She did not include full grade levels or require workshops or summer reading. She simply said she would support this professional learning opportunity for these two successful teachers who had uncovered a professional need and craved professional learning that was unique to that need. Both teachers agreed they wanted to pursue this professional learning. From there, two Host Teachers were born.

By noticing and supporting the professional values of lifelong learning and authenticity, the principal was able to combine the exploration of data with this value-driven work. Both teachers wanted to improve. They wanted to grow and serve their students in a different way. While the conversations at the school level started with data, it organically shifted into value work.

Both teachers, Ms. Salinas and Mrs. Morrigan, were thrilled to have a tailored opportunity for professional learning. Together with the principal, the teachers agreed their goals would be to focus on making small groups more responsive based on their data. By this time, there was more data than what had been noticed over the summer. Now they had real-time data of students from required statewide check-ins and observational data from the classwork. They dug deeply into this new information and started to consider next steps.

From there, the teachers developed a Continuum of Practice for small flexible groups for their content areas (Appendix 2 shows the ELA example) alongside their ERG consultant. These documents helped determine where they were with their practices and where they wanted to be. The large goal of the project included having small groups in place twice a week by the end of the semester. We encourage schools to set qualitative goals in order to measure progress along the way instead of only waiting for quantitative student data from external sources. Within each large goal, the teachers set their own personal goals for first and second quarter respectively. Both teachers determined they were in the Foundation Stage and wanted support with students working independently. The specific indicators in the Foundation Stage included having students begin meaningful independent work and problem solve independently during this time. In addition, teachers would model processes and procedures as well as provide guidance and feedback to increase stamina during this time. These are concrete, observable indicators that can be easily identified and more importantly, celebrated. Once the goals were set, the plan included a learning opportunity along with three observation and feedback sessions.

This particular project was very fluid because the Host Teachers immediately took ownership of data and expressed a need and then took a deeper dive once they had been selected as Host Teachers. Because of the organic nature of this project, the principal was able to leverage momentum from conversations to naturally and quickly identify the Host Teachers.

High School Case Study: Bailey High School

In our experience, high school teachers can be reluctant to ask for professional development, and this can be a challenge for instructional leaders and principals who need to make the case for change. In one of our high schools, there is a principal who is a true instructional leader. He prioritizes and focuses on improving teaching and learning within a school by establishing a vision, using data to guide decisions, providing ongoing coaching and professional development for teachers, and ensuring a student-centered environment where learning is the ultimate goal. He attends department meetings, knows students by name, and truly wants success for all within his building.

When he noticed teachers were working hard but not examining student work, he pulled in his administration team to discuss. From that conversation, he selected one of the assistant principals, Ms. Harold, to be an internal school Support Leader of professional learning. From there, he and the Support Leader started conversations to gather information about teacher mindset and beliefs around professional learning. Through these conversations, Ms. Harold helped her teachers reflect on their mindsets around professional learning and consider how ready they were to begin a Follow Me Forward journey. Some teachers at that point opted out.

They did not have the bandwidth to manage their outside-the-classroom coaching and club duties with another mental task. A few teachers were struggling with the basics of teaching and wanted to be more stable with classroom management before they committed to a larger project. These are both examples of real school and make the case for invitational professional learning work. If participants are not ready to engage in the change process, then the professional learning is wasted. The teachers who opted out were not penalized. These teachers simply were not yet starting on the Follow Me Forward path.

Ultimately, the school invited two teachers into this new professional learning initiative, and they became Host Teachers. One was a veteran, and one was just a few years into teaching. They were from different departments, but each of them wanted to deepen their understanding of student thinking and sharpen their skills for being responsive to student learning. The important thing they had in common was a desire to learn and grow as professionals.

These Host Teachers and Support Leader started to comb through various data points. While already content experts, their conversations highlighted a need for responsive teaching in all classes. In order to do this, teachers had to begin assigning work that showed more student thinking and take time to examine it through collaborative conversations. The goals included a closer examination of tasks and how student success criteria could be established within lessons in order to show understanding.

At the end of the collaborative meetings and goal-setting, the school arranged for ERG to provide the next steps for teachers and lead the plan moving forward. A Continuum of Practice for was developed, and the stage was set for implementation.

Summary

Phase 1 addresses values and beliefs of professional learning and is the beginning of a five-phase learning loop. The anchor tool *Making the Shift: Values and Beliefs About Professional Learning* enables all stakeholders to examine their values and beliefs, set personal goals, and take ownership of their learning experience. This anchor tool will be revisited as host teachers move along in the phases.

Other key actions in Phase 1 include identifying a Support Leader and extending an invitation to Host Teachers. Both the Support Leader and Host Teachers should value life-long learning, authenticity, and belonging and believe in curiosity, collaboration, and creating meaning.

Follow Me Forward encourages Host Teachers to discern needs through holistic data, such as classroom observations, anecdotal notes, and examining student work to understand thinking rather than giving a grade. Goals are set and a Continuum of Practice is developed to help guide the Host Teachers through the Foundation, Expansion, and Refinement stages as they work to achieve the goals.

CHAPTER 4

Phase 2:
Build Capacity with Host Teachers

Overview of Phase 2

1. Implement a Learning Opportunity for Host Teachers
2. Demonstrate a Lesson for Host Teachers
3. Provide Three Support Sessions for Host Teachers

Step 1: Implement a Learning Opportunity for Host Teachers

In Phase 2, Host Teachers step into active learning designed around the goals identified in Phase 1. These learning opportunities are not one-size-fits-all. Instead, they are carefully designed with the Support Leader to match the goals Host Teachers cocreated earlier. The format can vary ranging from book studies, research reviews, or expert-led sessions. However, the unifying thread is that each opportunity is purposeful, relevant, and tied directly to the established goals. By starting here, Host Teachers become equipped with capacity needed to move forward.

Step 2: Demonstrate a Lesson for Host Teachers

Next, the Support Leader models practice in action. A demonstration lesson is delivered in the Host Teacher classroom, aligned directly to the goals set in Phase 1. The purpose is not to provide a perfect model, but rather a live example of what it looks like to bring the goals to life through instruction. This demonstration step enables Host Teachers to observe, question, and analyze instructional choices in real time, making the goals more concrete and attainable. The demonstration serves as a bridge between theory and practice.

Step 3: Provide Three Support Sessions for Host Teachers

Finally, Host Teachers begin to practice on their own. In three structured support sessions, Host Teachers teach lessons aligned with their Phase 1 goals while the Support Leader observes. Feedback is delivered in a strength-based, growth-oriented manner. These sessions are not evaluations; they are capacity-building experiences. With each support session, Host Teachers refine their craft, gain confidence, and begin to internalize the new practices.

Step 1: Implement a Learning Opportunity for Host Teachers

There is no single format for this professional learning opportunity, but it should be meaningful, collaborative, and relevant to the instructional goals set in Phase 1. The initial learning experience is critical. It sets the stage for implementation of the goals set in Phase 1. These learning opportunities can take many forms:

- **Book studies** tied to the instructional shift or set of content goals
- **Research reviews** grounded in best practices and evidence-based strategies
- **Expert-led sessions** with specialists who can deepen teacher knowledge (e.g., hiring a Guided Math consultant when implementing small-group math instruction)

Follow Me Forward Story

In Phase 1, Alice and the two seventh-grade ELA teachers set a shared goal: to strengthen productive small-group instruction. As they looked ahead, two specific concerns surfaced.

First, the teachers were uncertain about what students not in a teacher-led group would be doing. They had never released students to independent work for extended periods and worried that this shift might mean "losing control" of their classrooms. Second, because they had previously relied on a mandated reading series, they were unsure about how to select appropriate texts for the small-group lessons.

To address these concerns, Alice designed a learning opportunity tailored to their needs. She gathered high-quality, research-based articles and identified credible websites that explored both independent work structures and small-group text selection. Teachers shared ideas that resonated with them from the materials. In addition, the teachers were able to share their misconceptions about independent work structures. One teacher had an "aha" moment when she realized the independent work did not have to be set up in concurrent small groups. Through reading and talking, she was able to build a new picture of what was possible in her classroom. In addition to considering a new approach, she was able to let go of strategies, resources, and approaches that no longer were relevant to her goals.

Step 2: Demonstrate a Lesson for Host Teachers

In the next step of the Follow Me Forward Model, most Host Teachers invite the Support Leader to teach a demonstration lesson. However, some middle and high school teachers prefer to skip this step, as having someone else lead their class can feel disruptive, and content may be extremely technical at the upper levels. In those cases, Host Teachers move directly into the three support sessions to receive strength-based feedback related to processes. We honor this preference whenever It's requested.

During a demonstration lesson, the Host Teachers will observe, and as they do so, they will need the cocreated Continuum of Practice in front of them. The experience can be both exhilarating and overwhelming. There are many things happening at once, and without a focused lens, it's easy to miss what matters. Having the Continuum of Practice in front of them enables the Host Teacher to take notes, hold onto ideas, and write questions to prepare for the face-to-face debrief.

Face-to-Face Debrief Conversation

A face-to-face debrief conversation should happen as soon as possible after the demonstration lesson. The Support Leader who demonstrates the lesson and the Host Teacher who observed the lesson are included. Although it may take getting class coverage, preferably the debrief happens right after the demonstration lesson. It can take place later in the day, but it is our recommendation that it *always* happens the day of the demonstration. The notes the Host Teacher took on the Continuum of Practice provide a structured starting point, anchoring the conversation in observed evidence. From there, the conversation can evolve into a more holistic, reflective and natural dialogue about the teaching and learning that occurred during the demonstration lesson.

Below are key elements of the debrief after the demonstration lesson:

- Discuss goal-aligned instruction and responsive teaching.
- Reflect on student engagement and evidence of learning.
- Pose and answer questions to clarify or deepen understanding.
- Share insights and next steps for applying what was observed.

Follow Me Forward Story

Continuing with the story of Alice working alongside two middle school ELA teachers who had set the goal of reducing whole-group instruction in favor of more intentional small-group learning. Together, they developed a Continuum of Practice to guide what high-quality small group lessons should look like in action. This tool became an anchor for their next steps.

When Alice entered each Host Teacher's classroom to demonstrate a lesson, the teacher had this Continuum of Practice in hand. As the lesson unfolded, the Host Teacher actively recorded observation and notes. This note-taking process gave the Host Teacher a focused lens through which to watch the demonstration instead of being distracted by other things happening within the course of a lesson.

Immediately following the demonstration, Alice and the Host Teacher engaged in a structured debrief conversation. By using the notes as a springboard for dialogue, the teacher was able to lead the conversation with what they noticed and what they had questions about. In addition, the teacher and Alice collaboratively reflected on the strengths of the lesson as well as different avenues for next steps. Together, Alice and the teacher decided on the goals for the support sessions using the Continuum of Practice as the guide.

Step 3: Provide Three Support Sessions for Host Teachers

Following the demonstration lesson, each Host Teacher receives three scheduled support sessions from the Support Leader. We recommend scheduling visits two to three weeks apart allowing time for the Host Teacher to digest and practice what is being learned. These visits are not old-fashioned unannounced pop-ins with a sticky note left on a teacher's desk. Instead, they are thoughtfully planned support sessions. We recommend a minimum of 45 minutes for elementary observations and at least 30 minutes for secondary, depending on how their master schedule works.

In *Why a Teacher's Belief Matters: Using a Theory of Learning to Explore Instructional Decisions* (2022), researcher Brian Cambourne emphasized that when learning something new, learners should not be required to wait until they have mastered it before applying it. Instead, they are encouraged to "have a go," to make an attempt at emulating what has been demonstrated. In our model of professional learning, this is the stage where teachers "have a go" with substantial, scaffolded support and guidance from the Support Leader.

Observing the Host Teacher

The Support Leader and the Host Teacher plan three different times for the Host Teacher to teach and the Support Leader to observe based on goals and the Continuum of Practice indicators that were cocreated. The Support Leader provides timely, high-level, strength-based feedback that helps the Host Teacher reflect, refine, and build confidence. The purpose of the support sessions is for the Host Teacher to practice and grow with expert support from the Support Leader.

Feedback is written like a conversation on paper. We recommend the feedback is written directly to the teacher so it is unique and supportive. Including the word "you" instead of "the teacher" personalizes the feedback and makes more sense as the teacher reads it.

Feedback is intentionally designed to promote teacher reflection, growth, and instructional clarity. When documenting observations and feedback, there are four essential components:

1. Scripting
2. Summary
3. Reflective questions
4. Helpful tips

Scripting

Scripting captures the actual dialogue or instructional moves observed during the lesson, enabling teachers to revisit what they said or did in context.

EXAMPLE 1:

You posed prompts that promoted student comprehension and thinking:
- "What are you learning?"
- "What are you inferring?"
- "What do you know now that you didn't know before reading this text?"

EXAMPLE 2:

Ms. A:	Do you understand that sentence?
Student:	No.
Ms. A:	Can you show me what is confusing you?
Student:	Yes. *(Points to the word – seized)*
	(You helped the student pronounce the word.)
Ms. A:	Have you heard that word?
Student:	No.
Ms. A:	So what do you think it might mean? Let's reread the sentence.
Student:	Like grabbed at her?
Ms. A:	Yes, that's right!

Summary

The summary provides a concise overview of the lesson events.

EXAMPLE 1: *You reviewed characteristics of nonfiction to prepare students for reading.*

EXAMPLE 2: *You assessed student background knowledge about the topic.*

Reflective questions

Reflective questions are open-ended prompts that promote teacher reflection on instructional choices and student responses.

EXAMPLE 1: *Reflect: What could you have done to get readers thinking about cause and effect before the lesson, as this was the stated purpose?*

EXAMPLE 2: *Reflect: How does this activity help your readers decode and comprehend the text?*

EXAMPLE 3: *Reflect: Students read with high accuracy. Is this text still at their instructional level, or are they ready for more challenges?*

Helpful tips

Helpful tips offer suggestions for improvement.

EXAMPLE 1: *Tip: Consider setting a clear purpose at the start of the lesson. For example:* "Today, as we're reading, we'll be making connections between the text and what we already know about ecosystems."

Follow Me Forward Story

Alice supported both ELA middle school teachers with three support sessions. Within each session, she observed them working with students in a small-group lesson at the teacher table. Before observing, Alice announced the date and time of the classroom visit and reminded teachers she would take notes on the cocreated Continuum of Practice. While observing, Alice made notes of what was going well within the lesson as well as possible next steps. After the observation, Alice talked with each teacher to collaboratively reflect and consider how the lesson went according to the Continuum of Practice. She was able to drive the conversation around the items on the Continuum so it was a focused and effective use of time. Teachers identified their own strengths and then their next steps. Together they considered how to move forward for each group. We have included one sample of the feedback Alice gave while working with teachers on productive small-group instruction, Appendix 3 in the back of this book. You can see her observer notes are specific to the indicators.

The Collaborative Debrief

After each observation support session, the Host Teacher and Support Leader engage in a timely coaching conversation, ideally the same day or within 24 hours. As with the debrief following a demonstration lesson, this discussion is most effective when it is structured, purposeful, and focused on reflection and growth. Without a clear framework, conversations can easily drift into unrelated topics or frustrations. A structured approach keeps the dialogue grounded in evidence, aligned with best practices, and centered on authenticity.

To guide these reflective discussions, Support Leaders use the *Collaborative Debrief Tool,* which provides prompts for a two-way, meaningful exchange. This tool reinforces shared ownership in the learning process ensuring both the Host Teacher and Support Leader contribute equally to reflection and next steps. The *Collaborative Debrief Tool* is discussed with the Host Teacher before the observation by the Support Leader, so the Host Teacher understands there is shared involvement in the conversation and they belong in the conversation just as much as the Support Leader. A sample of the *Collaborative Debrief Tool* is provided below and in the Appendices section of this book (Appendix 4).

Collaborative Debrief Tool

To guide a reflective, two-way conversation after a lesson.

	Support Leader Brings	**Host Teacher Brings**
Stance & Focus	• A stance of curiosity, not judgment— asking probing questions to understand the teacher's perspective. • Noticings about student engagement, pacing, and alignment with intended goals. • Affirmation that validates the teacher's self-assessment and learning. **Sample Questions:** – What part of the lesson felt most alive to you? – What surprised you about student responses?	• Honest reflection about what worked and what surprised them. • Evidence of student engagement or learning (student work samples, comments, or observed behaviors). • Awareness of emotional and instructional moments that stood out during the lesson.

	Support Leader Brings	Host Teacher Brings
Goal Connection & Clarification	• Connection back to the goal set in the Continuum of Learning. • Prompts that unpack the learning intention (e.g., "What thinking did you hope to see?"). • Clarifying questions to help identify the targeted skill, strategy, or behavior. **Sample Questions:** – What thinking did you hope to see? – How did you communicate the goal to students? – What did you notice students doing that reflected progress toward the goal?	• Description of how the goal was communicated to students. • Reflections on whether students met expectations or need additional scaffolding.
Interpretation & Guidance	• Encouragement to interpret student evidence rather than evaluate teaching. • Curiosity about what the teacher noticed in the moment. • Guidance that connects observations to next instructional steps. **Sample Questions:** – What patterns do you see in student responses? – How do these insights inform what comes next? – What might you adjust or keep the same next time?	• Specific examples of what students said, did, or produced. • Insights into student readiness, engagement, or misconceptions. • Reflection on how these insights might shape upcoming instruction.

	Support Leader Brings	Host Teacher Brings
Next Steps & Support	• One actionable suggestion aligned with the teacher's goal. • Offer of support—resources, modeling, or collaboration if requested. **Sample Questions:** – What do you see as your next action step? – What kind of support feels most useful right now?	• Personal takeaway or small action step for continued growth. • Reflections on what support or feedback would be most helpful moving forward.

The *Continuum of Practice with Feedback* (Appendix 3) and the *Collaborative Debrief Tool* (Appendix 4) work together to support focused, high-level coaching conversations between the Host Teacher and Support Leader. Used during the three support sessions in Phase 2, these tools build instructional capacity and guide professional growth. After each debrief, the Support Leader documents next steps, lesson highlights, and cocreated goals, then shares the completed form with the Host Teacher. This record provides an ongoing reference for reflection, feedback, and growth.

Elementary Case Study: Franklin Elementary School

Franklin Elementary school's journey into Phase 2 began with a strong foundation: a two-day training focused on small-group instruction provided by an expert in small-group math. After the training, the ERG Support Leader did a small-group math demonstration lesson in each of the three Host Teacher classrooms.

This live modeling served as a catalyst for implementation, enabling Host Teachers to see theory come to life and easing the natural anxiety. By witnessing effective small-group math instruction firsthand and seeing it happen with their own students, Host Teachers felt more confident and prepared to try themselves.

After the demonstration lesson, the focus shifted from observing others to refining their instruction. Each Host Teacher participated in three support sessions again with a Support Leader from ERG—a critical structure that emphasized support, not evaluation.

A detailed schedule ensured that each teacher received three rounds of embedded support sessions. Each cycle included an observation during a small-group math lesson followed by a debrief session focused on goals for next steps.

The support sessions were structured in a two-way conversation that enables the Host Teacher to be heard and gradually build expertise and confidence in the small-group math framework.

Only after completing three full support sessions did the Host Teachers begin to prepare their mindsets to welcome visiting peers into their authentic classrooms. This intentional sequencing ensured that teachers felt prepared and supported before inviting colleagues in to learn with them..

Middle School Case Study: West End Middle School

Because the teachers involved at West End Middle School were in different grades and different subjects, the learning opportunities were unique to them. One teacher elected to have a demonstration lesson as a way to increase the understanding while another teacher chose a research article as the first step toward building capacity. Both teachers were involved in the creation of benchmarks related to small-group instruction and received three support sessions that included focused observations and feedback from the ERG consultant.

Ms. Salinas, a math teacher, had extensive background in working with small groups. She did not feel like she needed any more information; she just needed help with application of ideas and fine-tuning her process to fit the time allowed in a sixth-grade math class. By choosing a research article and her own learning path, she was very engaged and immediately took ownership of the learning process. She knew her pitfalls from prior years and asked for her feedback to be focused on pacing, teacher talk, and planning next steps. Using the *Continuum of Practice* for small-group math, along with the article, Ms. Salinas rapidly moved into the Expansion phase. By becoming a partner in the learning, the consultant provided specific information for Ms. Salinas who in turn, was able to come up with her own solutions and keep moving forward.

Mrs. Morrigan was recently certified to teach English language arts. She had experience in the classroom but wanted a demonstration lesson since her background was not as vast and it helped to "see and hear" what was possible in the small group. Using the collaboratively designed *Continuum of Practice* (Appendix 2), the ERG consultant and Mrs. Morrigan planned a lesson together that aligned with the specific standards she was working on along with text that would be successful for her students. During the demonstration lesson, Mrs. Morrigan took extensive notes on what she saw and jotted questions that were discussed in a focused and productive debrief conversation. The coaching conversation enabled Mrs. Morrigan to confirm her ideas about the demonstration lesson and ask her authentic questions in a safe space. By choosing her specific learning opportunity, Ms. Morrigan transformed her overwhelm to excitement. She could not wait to jump in and try what she had learned as soon as possible.

Both Ms. Salinas and Mrs. Morrigan scheduled three follow-up observation and feedback sessions with the ERG consultant. The sample of Mrs. Morrigan's notes are included in *Continuum of Practice with Feedback* (Appendix 3) at the back of this text. By demonstrating a lesson and staying focused on the Continuum of Practice to provide feedback, each teacher clearly understood where they were and where they were headed.

High School Case Study: Bailey High School

At the high school, the initial learning opportunities took place in planning time. It is often difficult to pull a variety of departments together, so the content was broken into small chunks and reviewed in short sessions across a few visits. A book study was used to anchor the work, so teachers could digest information between visits from the ERG consultant.

The result of this approach enabled teachers from both the Biology and History departments to participate in the project without having to meet before or after school hours. Not having an "add on" was much more conducive for the schedule of a busy high school teacher. The short, focused conversations anchored with a text helped keep things moving forward without causing major disruptions to other responsibilities and duties that are commonplace in high schools. Instead of demonstration lessons, the Host Teachers elected to jump right into their observation sessions using their Continuum of Practice.

The three follow-up observation and support sessions were essential for the high school teachers and became an avenue for swift growth. Ms. Carmen was able to quickly apply ideas and through reflection, identify specific areas of need. The ERG consultant focused the feedback on these self-identified areas and also followed up with planning support that related to alignment of standards with activities. "I had been using this activity for years, but when I started questioning how I assessed it, I realized I needed to make a few changes," she said.

Without reflecting and being asked key questions in the coaching conversation aligned with the Continuum of Practice, this revelation would not have been possible."

Ms. Woods was also able to quickly take the ideas and include them in her lesson plans. The observation and feedback sessions were particularly useful for Ms. Woods, who understood the ideas but was having a difficult time with application in real time. Her students were at risk and very challenging. The three observation and support sessions were critical to keep Ms. Woods encouraged and provide her with a thinking partner at incremental stages of the semester. Ms. Woods particularly enjoyed the coaching conversations as ways to discuss what was working based on the Continuum of Practice and also problem solve some of the barriers in her classroom.

Summary

Phase 2 of the Follow Me Forward Model is a high-leverage stage where professional learning shifts from ideas to action. It begins once Host Teachers step onto the path with a Support Leader guiding the way. Momentum builds through three authentic, intentional actions including a learning opportunity, a demonstration lesson, and three structured support sessions enriched with strength-based feedback.

The goals established in Phase 1 and the Continuum of Practice become the anchor for this work. They are modeled during the demonstration lesson, so Host Teachers can see what indicators look and sound like in practice. These same goals and Continuum of Practice then guide the support sessions, ensuring consistency and alignment with authentic, student-centered instruction.

As the Host Teacher and Support Leader collaborate and engage in meaningful interactions, a genuine sense of belonging grows stronger. Phase 2 is where confidence grows, skills deepen, and professional learning becomes visible, shared, and actionable.

CHAPTER 5

Phase 3:
Practice, Self-Reflect, and Polish

Overview of Phase 3

1. Absorb and Reflect
2. Self-reflect Through Video
3. Prepare for Visitors

Step 1: Absorb and Reflect

Phase 3 marks a turning point for Host Teachers. After walking closely with their Support Leader in Phase 2, they begin to absorb what they have learned and move into a rhythm of practice, self-reflection, and polish. The Support Leader does not disappear but shifts into a more responsive role and is available as needed and when requested. This is the phase where Host Teachers begin to internalize their learning and make it their own.

Step 2: Self-Reflect Through Video

A meaningful feature of Phase 3 is the use of video for self-observation. When teachers record their own lessons, the invisible becomes visible. The video serves as a mirror, revealing patterns in instruction that might otherwise go unnoticed. Watching and reflecting on our own practice sharpens decision-making, highlights strengths, and provides a safe space to analyze areas for growth. Over time, this practice builds confidence and deepens professional insight.

Step 3: Prepare for Visitors

Phase 3 is also a pivotal time of preparation. Soon, colleagues will arrive as visitors in Phase 4 with genuine curiosity and a desire to learn. Anticipating their questions helps Host Teachers not only refine the *what* and *how* of their instruction but also to reconnect with the deeper *why*. This readiness sets the stage for a powerful shift: moving from private reflection to collaboration with peers.

Step 1: Absorb and Reflect

In Phase 3 of the Follow Me Forward Model, teachers absorb what they learned in Phase 2. They move into a rhythm of practice, self-reflection, and polish with less formal support from the Support Leader. However, the Support Leader still guides and lights the way for Host Teachers so that the sense of belonging remains strong.

In this phase support from the Support Leader is as needed and when requested. For example, during this stage one Host Teacher wanted to give better feedback to students during one on one conferences, so the Host Teacher invited the Support Leader in to demonstrate some one on one conference techniques. The goal is never perfection of teaching but steady growth in building capacity.

As discussed in Phase 2, Brian Cambourne's concept of *approximations* is central here. When toddlers are learning to walk, every attempt, no matter how imperfect, is celebrated. They stand, wobble, fall, try again, and eventually take their first steps. We don't expect mastery on day one. Instead, we value progress and perseverance. The same is true for Host Teachers. Lessons may not always unfold as planned, but every attempt provides valuable insight in an authentic process of learning by doing.

Rodes and Melville, in their article *Taking Risks with Rough Draft Teaching*, remind us that "one could argue that the heart of the lesson is what occurs after a lesson has been taught." This phase embraces that truth. Host Teachers are encouraged to practice, self-reflect, and polish—repeating as often as needed. As self efficacy grows, Host Teachers open their classrooms to peers, expanding opportunities for collective learning, including but not limited to, Phase 4.

Again, coaching conversations and reflection with the Support Leaders continue throughout Phase 3 as needed. The support provided by the Support Leader could be email check-ins, virtual sessions, and classroom visits. For consistency, the Support Leader within the school or the external consultant such as ERG follow the Host Teacher across the phases including this one even though responsibility is being released.

Step 2: Self Reflect Through Video

In Phase 3, Host Teachers incorporate self-observation through video reflection. Teachers can gain powerful insights by watching themselves in action. They can also learn by observing their students from a more neutral perspective. This practice is similar to the review of film footage when football players run to the sideline to review or golfers adjust their swing after a film session. For athletes, film transforms invisible habits into visible data. It becomes a mirror for performance, helping refine technique, sharpen decision-making, and build confidence. The same is true for teachers. A short video clip can highlight strengths, reveal missed opportunities, and spark ideas for immediate improvement with teaching and learning.

This meaningful process of filming gives learners, in this case teachers, another chance to practice, self-reflect, and polish. And because video reflection can be done anytime, it offers autonomy. Teachers may review their video on their own or choose to invite a colleague or the Support Leader into the process. It is completely their choice. Reflection or notation forms are not needed for this step. This is a straightforward simple process of turning on a camera during a lesson aligned with goals and watching it at a later time. The purpose is to promote growth of instructional practice. Recording and playback help learners by offering clarity, evidence, feedback and self-awareness to the teacher. These are essential ingredients for growth when learning anything for the first time.

Step 3: Prepare for Visitors

In Phase 4, the Host Teacher invites colleagues into the classroom to observe authentic teaching and learning. This is not a quick pop-in to jot down "wows" and "wonders," nor is it the same as a casual learning walk. Host Teachers utilize this part of Phase 3 to prepare for the visits.

When colleagues visit a Host Teacher's classroom, the focus is purposeful. They observe the teaching and learning taking place live in the Host Teacher Classroom and participate in a professional debrief conversation with the Host Teacher. This makes Phase 3 a pivotal stage for the Host Teacher to reflect deeply on both the what, how, and why of their instruction. Visitors arrive with genuine curiosity, so anticipating their questions is key. During this time of absorption it is necessary for teachers to anticipate the questions visitors will have after observing.

It is not uncommon for teachers to have knowledge and expertise while also having difficulty articulating their practice. Because of this, the Support Leader sits with Host Teachers and role-plays the following questions as a way to prepare the Host Teachers for visitors. In our field work and time spent with the Follow Me Forward Model, we have tracked some common trends of what visiting teachers are curious about and provided them below.

1. **Questions About the "What"**

- How did you decide on this focus for today?
- How do you know this is the right starting point for your students?

2. **Questions About the "How"**

- How did you decide which students to group together?
- What materials or resources are you using, and why?
- What routines or structures help your students work independently?
- How do you check for understanding in real time?

3. **Questions About the "Why"**

- Why did you choose this instructional strategy over another one?
- What data or observations influenced your planning?
- Why did you adjust (or not adjust) during the lesson?

4. **Reflective or Behind-the-Scenes Questions**

- What challenges have you encountered with this strategy?
- What systems help you manage materials and pacing?

Elementary Case Study: Franklin Elementary School

Teachers, like all learners, differ in how they process and apply new knowledge. Once the Follow Me Forward Model was underway at Franklin Elementary School, and the three support sessions were complete, clear patterns began to emerge, revealing what each teacher needed to deepen, extend, and refine their practice in teaching small, differentiated math groups.

By this stage, the three participating teachers were on different trajectories:

- Ms. Hardy used the *Continuum of Practice* to self-reflect and video-taped herself for authentic feedback. She had grown confident and was well on her way to opening her classroom for peer observation, eager to learn together with colleagues.
- Ms. Greg decided to leave the teaching profession altogether (for reasons unrelated to her role as a Host Teacher).
- Mr. Burns struggled to see how the math strategies aligned with district and school goals, perceiving them as "add-ons" rather than integral instructional practices.

This divergence illuminated two critical factors for success within the Follow Me Forward experience:

1. Determining the right teachers to serve as Host Teachers is paramount. Educators who are open, collaborative, and ready to embrace new approaches and take risks thrive within this model.
2. Clearly communicating the role and expectations of the Host Teacher from the beginning is important. Host Teachers need to understand how the work connects to broader school and district priorities. Taking time to clear up any misconceptions early on in the learning journey helps this phase go well.

Even the most thoughtfully designed professional learning initiative will take root differently in each teacher's practice. The Follow Me Forward Model reminds us that the path to lasting instructional change begins with people. Determining the right people to lead the way is just the beginning and evolves as they are supported with clarity and purpose to create conditions where growth is both possible and celebrated.

Middle School Case Study: West End Middle School

The West End Middle School teachers we worked with enjoyed the fluidity of this phase. Each teacher spent time practicing and reflecting and fine-tuning their instructional moves. When they requested an ERG consultant to observe, it was a lively conversation about what is working and what needs attention. It was also about celebrating their professionalism and students' progress.

Ms. Salinas was finally able to pace her lesson the way she wanted, so she could get two different small groups into the time frame along with a brief whole-group lesson. Because of her practice and reflection, she was much more aware of how she was using the time within each class period. With one small adjustment (using a timer), she had become very efficient and was building momentum. Her groups were now smoothly running two days a week, and students were consistently sustaining twenty to forty minutes of meaningful independent work. What she once thought was impossible was now happening on a regular basis. Having the support sessions enabled her to not only reflect on what was going well, but what she had done to create those conditions. Being consistent during this phase helped her solidify this practice and prepare for visitors. This absorption and reflection helped move Ms. Salinas through the expansion stage on the Continuum of Practice into the Refinement stage.

Mrs. Morrigan was also rapidly building momentum in this phase and had moved into the Expansion Stage on the Continuum of Practice. Her small groups were in place, students were working well independently, and she was digging into the curriculum in a way she had never imagined. Then she hit a barrier. It snowed, so kids were out of school for a few days. The routines fell apart, and suddenly students were coming to her small groups unprepared. She bravely voiced these concerns in one of her support sessions after a particularly bumpy lesson. With the help of her Support Leader (an ERG consultant), she was able to consider some alternative approaches as she worked to support students through the end of the unit of study. In this case, her willingness to collaborate and continually try new things helped revitalize her small-group work, which ultimately led to success.

At the end of this phase, Ms Salinas and Ms. Morrigan sat down together to talk about the upcoming visits to their classrooms. Their Support Leader (an ERG consultant) discussed expectations and answered questions so everyone was at ease prior to the visits. Part of that conversation included looking back at where they started and where they were on the Continuum of Practice. Both teachers shared how their reluctance at the beginning transformed once they began the work. They were extremely proud of their practice and how they were showing up in the classroom and looked forward to sharing this with visitors.

High School Case Study: Bailey High School

At the high school, this phase of the work was some of the most difficult but also the most rewarding. Ms. Carmen continued to integrate the assessment practices into her lessons and reconsider assignments with a new lens. She liked the way this helped her see students in a different light and also forced her to consider why she was making the instructional decisions she made. The feedback and conversations with her Support Leader helped her become aware, intentional, and more focused. She moved from the Foundation Stage on the Continuum of Practice into the Expansion Stage and was well on her way into the Refinement work.

Ms. Woods on the other hand found some of the ideas difficult to implement. She could understand many of the formative assessment ideas but was struggling to apply them consistently. She found herself on the border of the Foundation and Expansion Stages on the Continuum of Practice. She was making progress, but she needed more time to practice before visitors came in to observe her working with students. After careful consideration and the visitor timeline, Ms. Woods agreed that she and her students were not ready for visitors.

Instead, Ms. Woods agreed to be on a panel discussion to help explain the Follow Me Forward Model and how it was changing her as she evolved as an educator. While Ms. Woods was not able to accept visitors during Phase 4, it is worth noting that Ms. Woods continued for the duration of the Follow Me Forward learning loop and was an integral part of the continuous learning loops and collaborative work.

The authenticity and vulnerability of Ms. Woods is one we wanted to highlight as part of the professional learning process. It is not uncommon when learning something new to initially walk away with an understanding of ideas and have difficulty with application when returning to the classroom. Sometimes it takes more time for one person to implement than another, and having awareness around this is important. Ms. Woods remained curious and was able to continue learning over time despite not having visitors into the classroom on the scheduled date. We see Ms. Woods as a success story for honoring the values and beliefs of the model and doing the hard work of transforming as an educator. Instead of abandoning the process or feeling defeated, Ms. Woods continued to learn at her own rate and into the Year 2 learning loop.

Summary

In Phase 3 of the Follow Me Forward Model, Host Teachers build on what they learned in Phase 2 through the learning opportunities, demonstration lesson, and three support sessions with strength-based feedback. They now enter a steady loop of authentic practice, reflection, and refinement, focusing on sustained growth rather than perfection. Guided by Brian Cambourne's concept of *approximations*, each teaching attempt, whether or not it is successful, is recognized as an important step in the learning process.

Host Teachers are encouraged to teach, self-reflect, and refine their approach, repeating this loop as often as needed. Ongoing meaningful coaching conversations with a Support Leader provide targeted support as requested by the Host Teacher. In this phase, video self-reflection helps teachers identify strengths, spot missed opportunities, and another opportunity to self-reflect, refine and polish and also foster curiosity about what is possible.

Phase 3 also prepares Host Teachers to welcome colleagues into their classrooms to learn through collaboration in Phase 4. Preparation involves building self efficacy through practice and anticipating visitor questions by role playing with the Support Leader.

CHAPTER 6

Phase 4: Immerse in Practice

Overview of Phase 4

1. Before the Visit to the Host Classroom
2. During the Visit to the Host Classroom
3. After the Visit to the Host Classroom

In Phase 4 of the Follow Me Forward journey, visitors are welcomed into the Host Teacher's classroom to observe live teaching in action. This is an immersion and experiential professional learning opportunity for both the Host Teacher and the visitors. The purpose is not to evaluate but to learn collaboratively. Visitors should be able to gain insight into instructional strategies, student engagement, and the natural flow of a lesson. The Host Teacher's lesson is aligned with the instructional goals that were determined collaboratively in Phase 1 and explicitly stated on the Continuum of Practice. For example, if goals were set to teach in productive small groups, when visitors are scheduled for observations in the Host Teacher's classroom, the lessons should align with the goals of productive small-group instruction.

Each Host Teacher is scheduled three different times for visits from peers, no more than five visitors at a time at each visit. In our field experience, we scheduled the visits approximately one month apart, which allows time for the Host Teacher to reset and reflect before the next group of visitors.

Step 1: Before the Visit to the Host Classroom

Two weeks prior to the classroom visit, the Support Leader and Host Teacher collaborate to schedule dates and identify up to five observers to offer invitations for visiting. On the day of the visit, the group gathers in a comfortable space such as the library, a conference room, or even a quiet hallway. This time is used to set the tone, review *What the Visit Is / What the Visit Is Not* (Appendix 5) and *Classroom Observation Tool*, and clarify expectations. Observers are reminded of the purpose of the visit and encouraged to ask questions before entering the classroom.

> **Bonus Resources:** For a downloadable copy of the *Classroom Observation Tool*, please visit www.myedresource.com.

Step 2: During the Visit to the Host Classroom

When the observation begins, visitors take on the role of quiet, attentive learners. They do not interact with students or the Host Teacher but instead focus on the flow of the lesson, teacher decisions, and evidence of student learning. Using *The Observation Tool*, they jot notes about what they notice, what they are curious about, and what might influence their own practice. The Support Leader remains present to anchor the experience, which typically lasts between forty-five and sixty minutes in elementary classrooms and a minimum of thirty minutes in secondary situations.

Step 3: After the Visit to the Host Classroom

Once the classroom portion concludes, observers gather again with the Support Leader for a short debrief. This step allows them to sort through their notes and refine their key takeaways, so the conversation remains professional and growth-oriented once the Host Teacher has joined. When the Host Teacher arrives, the discussion becomes a collegial exchange of questions, insights, and curiosities. The conversation honors the Host Teacher's expertise while enabling all participants to learn from one another. Before leaving, observers are invited to reflect on how the experience felt and how it will influence their teaching practice moving forward.

The Role of the Support Leader

We must point out the significance of the Support Leader role in this phase. In fact, the role of the Support Leader can make or break Phase 4 and the visit to Host Teacher classrooms. Historically, when teachers visit each other's classrooms, they are there to write wows and wonders and/or tell their colleagues the myriad of things they did right. The Follow Me Forward Model defines teacher-to-teacher classroom visits differently, and the Support Leader is a key factor in guiding this mindset during Phase 4. Instead of superficial or surface-level observations and comments, the expectation is that observers take a deep and meaningful dive into teaching and learning.

To ensure the visit to Host Teacher classrooms are as productive as possible, the Support Leaders meet with visitors/observers both before and after the classroom experience. The meeting before the observation provides an opportunity to clarify expectations, review observation tools, and align on the purpose of the visit. The post-visit conversation creates space for reflection, reveals shared insights, and demonstrates professional dialogue, setting the stage for meaningful, collaborative growth for both the Host Teacher and the observers. It is also a time to reflect on the experiential opportunity for learning. The Support Leader needs to be able to set this tone before, during, and after the visits.

Step 1: Before the Visit to the Host Classroom

At least two weeks before the visit takes place, dates should be scheduled in collaboration with the Host Teacher, including a shared decision about who will be visiting and observing. To maintain a focused and productive environment, we recommended that no more than five people participate in the observation. The five visitors may be other Host Teachers, teachers who are not Host Teachers in the school, or in some cases teachers from other schools.

In our field work we meet the visitors/observers in a cozy space in the library or an available conference room before the visit begins and after the visit concludes. Any space that will accommodate a collaborative conversation will work even if you need to stand in a comfortable circle in a quiet hallway. This is the time to set the tone for the visit and review protocols, etc.

Appendix 5 is included in the back of this text.

What the Visit to a Host Classroom Is	What the Visit to a Host Classroom Is Not
A time to learn from a peer	Letting your peer know what they did well and what they need to improve
Time to be a part of a schoolwide culture of curiosity, collaboration, and meaning	Expecting a perfect result from the lesson
A process for better understanding student learning and how to meet their needs	Passing blame on students or others when lessons are not perfect
A journey to continually improve one's teaching practice	Self-assessing one's or others' worth as a teacher
An opportunity to engage in experiential professional learning	A chance to get out of teaching in your classroom

During the gathering before entering the Host Teachers room, it is important for the Support Leader to explicitly state expectations around what to observe. The Support Leader shares a brief overview of the goals the Host Teacher has been working on and a brief description of the Continuum of Practice.

Using the above chart, the Support Leader discusses what the visit is and that the visit is not. In addition, each observer receives a copy of the *Classroom Visit Observation Tool*. The notes taken on this form will be used to guide a professional conversation following the observation. The note-taking form provides broad questions to provoke thinking and reflection about teaching and learning, as well as the process for professional learning.

- What did you notice about the climate of the classroom?
- What did you notice about the teaching?

- What did you notice about the learning?
- What teaching strategies did you observe?
- What evidence of student learning did you see?
- What are you curious about?
- What impact will this observation have on your teaching
- How has this type of professional learning helped you grow?

These two tools, *What the Visit Is / What the Visit Is Not* (Appendix 5) and the *Classroom Visit Observation Tool* can be sent to the observers ahead of time or given at the meeting before going into the classroom for the visit. Whether they are sent ahead of time or given on the day of the visit, the tools should be reviewed in person, and observers should be given a chance to ask questions for clarification. It is important not to skip this step before the observation. This step is the cornerstone of a successful, high-level visit to the Host Teacher classroom.

Bonus Resources: For a downloadable copy of the *Classroom Visit Observation Tool*, please visit www.myedresource.com.

Step 2: During the Visit to the Host Classroom

During the visit, observers remain in the role of quiet, attentive learners. They do not interact with students but instead focus on the work students are producing and the thinking that is taking place. Similarly, observers do not engage with the teacher during the lesson; their role is to watch and listen, concentrating on the flow of teaching and learning in the classroom, as well as teacher moves and decisions. Observers take notes on their observation tool, along with questions and areas of interest.

While the focus naturally includes observing the teacher's instructional moves, equal attention is given to how students are engaging with the lesson. Observers look for the connections between teaching and learning. They consider how the teacher's actions influence student understanding and how students respond to the tasks and questions presented. We recommend a forty-five to sixty minute time frame for the visit in the Host Teacher classroom for elementary schools and a minimum of thirty minutes for secondary. The Support Leader is in the observation classroom to see the experience firsthand and properly guide the debrief after the visit.

Step 3: After the Visit to the Host Classroom

Once the classroom observation concludes, the observers gather with the Support Leader who is guiding the visit for a brief pre-debriefing before the Host Teacher joins them. This time is used to review their notes, clarify key takeaways, and ensure that the feedback they will share is constructive, relevant, and suitable for professional dialogue. This is the time to vet any observation or comment that is not pertinent to a high-level conversation such as "two students were off task" or "one student had his hoodie on." While these might be factual observations, they are not necessarily relevant to the goals or indicators on the Continuum of Practice. It is important to redirect the observers as needed to the teaching and learning focus.

When the Host Teacher joins the group, the conversation shifts into a collaborative exchange. The tone is natural and collegial, with observers asking thoughtful questions, sharing insights, and voicing their curiosities. The discussion is anchored in what was seen and heard during the visit, with the shared goal of deepening professional practice. This process not only honors the growing expertise of the Host Teacher but also creates a space where all participants learn from one another with a sense of belonging. The Host Teacher may have the opportunity to share with the group more about the Continuum of Practice with the visitors. Before the group disperses, participants are invited to share how the experiential professional learning experience felt for them. Encourage them to articulate how the immersion experience will influence their growth as a teacher, both in their immediate classroom practice and in their long-term professional journey. By doing this, we continue to promote the values of lifelong learning, belonging and authenticity.

Elementary Case Study: Franklin Elementary School

The one Host Teacher at Franklin Elementary School who emerged as a leader was Ms. Hardy. She embraced the opportunity to open her classroom and was genuinely excited to have visitors observe her teaching. Her self-efficacy was on the rise, and so the visits began.

Small groups of five teachers were invited at a time to observe Ms. Hardy in action. Before each visit, the observers met with the Support Leader (an ERG consultant) at a table in the library of the school. Expectations were clearly outlined. For example, observers were encouraged to focus on teaching and learning rather than engaging in conversations with students that might disrupt instruction. An observation tool was provided to the observers to help them stay focused on teaching, learning, and student work.

After the classroom observation, Ms. Hardy met with the observer group to answer questions and engage in a reflective dialogue. These debriefing sessions enabled the sharing of insights, clarification, and a deeper understanding of the instructional strategies in action and the effectiveness of the Continuum of Practice.

Between January and April, three groups of five teachers each participated in this observation process. One key takeaway was that the post-observation reflection was essential for deepening learning and supporting the growth of all participants.

The Follow Me Forward experience was a resounding success at Franklin Elementary School. Both Ms. Hardy and the principal expressed enthusiasm about the culture of continual learning that took shape during this experience. When Ms. Hardy was invited to share her reflections, here's what she had to say:

"It has been a privilege to work directly with my colleagues as a Host Teacher and inspire them to try new methods when delivering lessons to students within their classrooms. This type of teacher-to-teacher professional learning is the best, in my opinion. It is teaching and learning in real time. Then, time is set aside for questions and conversations. It was a positive experience for all who participated. I am honored to have been a part."

Middle School Case Study: West End Middle School

When the day came for the first round of visitors at West End Middle School, the Host Teachers were very excited. They had worked very hard, and it felt exciting to have colleagues who wanted to watch and learn join the classroom. Both Ms. Salinas and Mrs. Morrigan thoughtfully prepared lessons and prepared the students, so regular instruction was not disrupted. They reviewed their Continuum of Practice, so they could effectively articulate their own journey through the indicators.

Prior to the visit, the Support Leader (an ERG consultant) talked with the visitors to establish basic ground rules. Visitors would use an observation form to watch and take focused notes. In addition to observing the teacher table, they could walk around and see what students were working on independently. The Support Leader clarified that the goal of the visit was not to interact with students, which is often a comfort zone of teachers. Instead, the goal was to observe teaching and learning, reflect, and walk away with next steps.

When teachers observed Ms. Salinas, they took notes, and in the conversation afterward, pointed out her pacing and her intentional planning, which was music to her ears. Because Ms. Salinas made it look so easy, several participants were not sure if they could "ever be that good." This was an important topic because instead of focusing on this final product of small groups, we helped visitors just focus on the one next step. Ms. Salinas was able to share where she started and encouraged the visitors to understand this had been an incremental journey. What they observed was not where she started. Ms. Salinas' authenticity helped teachers see themselves in the work. As a result the visitors went back to their classrooms to put their first steps into action. It was that simple. Adjusting the room arrangement and furniture for the small group was the gateway to moving forward with more small-group work.

For the observations in Mrs. Morrigan's room, visitors focused on the teacher table and also walked around to see what independent work students were engaged in. Visitors took notes and jotted questions to ask in our collaborative conversations. One of the largest takeaways from their observation was that it is important to start small. What teachers observed in the lesson was the result of weeks of work. Mrs. Morrigan did not start out with everything in place. She had incrementally put processes and procedures in place, so she and the students could be successful. She shared her own successes and pitfalls across the process and modeled lifelong learning as a teacher who was tackling a new subject. Talking this through with the group of visitors helped create belonging, and everyone determined a starting point for their own journey.

High School Case Study: Bailey High School

When the time came to visit the Bailey High School classrooms, Ms. Carmen checked in briefly with the Support Leader (an ERG consultant) to review materials and the lesson plan a few days before the planned visit. This work before the visit is key for a productive and useful experience for visitors. On the morning of the visit, while Ms. Carmen was with her students, the visitors gathered in a meeting room as a group and discussed the project and the purpose of the visit. This brief but powerful interaction helped keep everyone on track during the visit. The observation forms guided focused observation and notes, and visitors were able to chat with each other and feel welcomed by the administration team. Students were also expecting visitors and had an understanding of what was appropriate and what was not during the visit.

The in-class observations went well, and the Support Leaders arranged for coverage for Ms. Carmen to participate in the reflective debrief conversations. Although Ms. Woods had elected not to have visitors in her classroom during this phase, she was included in the collaborative professional conversation after the observation. This was important because she could still share her professional journey, her thinking around the Follow Me Forward work, and her deepening understanding of assessment. In addition, she could talk about the Continuum of Practice and how she had been digging in to solidify the work in the Expansion phase. Ms. Woods' authenticity in this conversation helped others recognize the personal nature of lifelong learning.

Ms. Carmen was particularly insightful when reflecting on the project and her own growth. "This is the most useful feedback I have gotten in seventeen years in the classroom. Applying the feedback, seeing results with kids, letting kids give feedback, and using the success criteria helped me streamline, not reinvent the wheel."

The result of these conversations was that teachers became energized. "How can we get this started in our classrooms?" was the most common question. Learning by observing real-life scenarios with real students was powerful and helped the visitors see themselves within the process, not outside of it. Belonging was organically created across the experience thanks to each teacher modeling lifelong learning and bringing authenticity to the conversations.

Summary

In Phase 4, Host Teachers open up their classrooms for live observations by colleagues, shifting professional learning from theory into shared, real-time practice in an experimental learning format. The Support Leader of the Follow Me Forward journey facilitates the process by meeting with observers before and after the visit to ensure clarity, focus, and a collegial tone.

Before the visit, details such as the date, participants, and purpose of the observation are agreed upon collaboratively. In order to be as productive and professional as possible, the visits to the host classroom are never a surprise.

Observers use a structured note-taking tool to capture evidence and insights, focusing on both teacher moves and student thinking. They also hear from the Support Leader what the visit is and what it is not. During the lesson, they maintain a quiet presence, engaging only through observation and taking notes on the note-taking form.

Afterward, observers meet briefly to organize their thoughts and refine their key takeaways before the Host Teacher joins. The debrief is a collaborative conversation where questions, insights, and curiosities are shared in a respectful, professional exchange. The goal is mutual learning and a sense of belonging. In addition, the dialogue results in strengthening instructional practice and promotes deep reflection on what next steps make sense for each participant.

CHAPTER 7

Phase 5: Reflect and Reset

Overview of Phase 5

1. Revisit Values and Beliefs
2. Reflect
3. Make a Commitment
4. Take Action

Step 1: Revisit Values and Beliefs

At the close of the Follow Me Forward journey, schools revisit the values and beliefs first identified in Phase 1. Using the *Making the Shift: Beliefs About Professional Learning* tool, teachers reflect on whether curiosity, collaboration, and meaning have deepened and whether their professional values have shifted, opening possibilities for lasting change.

Step 2: Reflect

Phase 5 is an intentional pause to assess impact. Reflection is not about vague impressions but specific insights connected to next steps. By examining all phases, teachers and leaders uncover lessons such as gaps in communication or support that guide stronger implementation in the future.

Step 3: Make a Commitment

Schools face a choice in Phase 5. They can stop after reflection or continue into an ongoing loop of professional growth. The Follow Me Forward Model calls for the latter path, where Host Teachers begin to grow exponentially as part of a sustainable model. They begin a new learning loop with new goals and deeper awareness and create momentum. New Host Teachers are considered, and the transformation of professional learning into a culture rather than a one-time event is underway.

Step 4: Take Action

The *Planning Tool for Year Two and Beyond* ensures insights turn into concrete next steps. By capturing learning and setting new goals, schools embed professional growth in a continuous loop, sustaining curiosity, collaboration, and meaning across years.

Step 1: Revisit Values and Beliefs

Now that a group of Host Teachers have made a learning loop through five phases with a Support Leader lighting the way, we can reflect on what we have accomplished on this full journey. We have explored values and beliefs, set goals, participated in a rich learning opportunity, observed a demonstration lesson, engaged in three support sessions, and opened Host classrooms on three different occasions to colleagues for authentic, collaborative learning. We set out with beliefs that the Follow Me Forward Model fosters curiosity, collaboration, and meaning, and these beliefs support the values of lifelong learning, authenticity, and belonging. We also set out on a collaborative path to lasting change. Now we reflect. Did we deepen or change our beliefs and values from Phase 1 to Phase 5? Have we made lasting change?

This is the time to revisit the *Making the Shift: Values and Beliefs About Professional Learning* inventory. By looking back at the beliefs recorded at the start of the path to lasting change, teachers and administrators can consider how their thinking has evolved throughout this experience. Has the learning process challenged old beliefs? Have new possibilities for professional learning emerged?

Phase 5 is the intentional pause in the Follow Me Forward journey. It is not the end; it is a pause. It is where teachers and leaders take time to reflect on their experiential learning, assess its impact on their practice and beliefs about professional learning, and set new goals to extend and deepen the work. This step transforms the actions from a single experience into an ongoing professional growth learning loop anchored in curiosity, collaboration, and meaning.

Step 2: Reflect

Professional reflection is the deliberate act of looking back on one's work to examine experiences, decisions, and outcomes to improve future practice. In the Follow Me Forward Model, this means pausing long enough to consider how values and beliefs, setting goals, learning opportunities, a demonstration lesson, support sessions, and classroom visits by peers have shaped not only what we do but who we have become.

Meaningful professional reflection moves beyond vague impressions such as, "The classroom visits were helpful," or "We need to explain Phase 4 better." Authentic reflection requires concrete, specific observations across all five phases that lead to actionable next steps.

For example, in one high school we partnered with, administrators began their first year of implementation by focusing on the English department, intentionally building a culture of embedded professional growth. At the end of that first year, the English department set aside time to reflect and consider the evolution of the work and themselves across the project. At the end of that reflection time, the English department agreed they wanted to continue the work into Year 2. At the same time, several Biology teachers had become interested in the work and expressed a desire to further their own professional learning by becoming Host Teachers in the coming year. The Biology department reviewed their own beliefs about lifelong learning, how to show up authentically and create belonging not just for the students, but across their department. After reflecting on their values and beliefs, two members of the biology department wanted to continue as Host Teachers, and the Support Leader at the school agreed this would be the logical next step. In Year 2, the English teachers became natural mentors for the Biology teachers who were developing as Host Teachers. As a group, they were able to immerse themselves in each other's classrooms while also welcoming new visitors as the project evolved. Professional reflection was an important support tool for these two groups as they continued to grow and learn. They had informal conversations with each other as well as protected time to check in on goals and problem-solve collaboratively as the school year progressed. Ultimately, teachers developed a larger sense of belonging as the initiative grew outside their own individual classrooms, and a self-sustaining culture was underway.

Step 3: Make a Commitment

Phase 5 represents a fork in the road. One path ends with reflection while the other continues toward ongoing learning. *Follow Me Forward* champions this second path, which is a continuous loop where teachers begin again with new goals and deeper insight. This approach ensures professional learning is not a single event but a living practice within the school, where teachers' voices and decision-making thrive.

If we stop at reflection, we risk letting this work be just another professional development box to check or something that earns CEUs but fades once it's done. That's not the intent of this model. *Follow Me Forward* is not a program with an endpoint; it is a living, continuous loop of learning designed for lasting change.

At this stage, the Support Leader's key question becomes, *What happens next?* Who will be the next group of Host Teachers and how can we sustain the important work of Year 1 Host Teachers? Much like looping with students, returning to the process brings valuable background knowledge, familiarity, and momentum. A Support Leader's role is to commit to light the path forward for new teachers beginning their first walk and for returning teachers who re-enter the loop with fresh goals and deeper awareness of what's possible through *Follow Me Forward*. By doing this, lifelong learning continues to take root within the school culture.

Step 4: Take Action

This is where the *Planning Tool for Year Two and Beyond* comes into play. The tool provides a structured way for schools to capture insights, set goals, and map out concrete next steps. It ensures that professional learning is not a one-time event but a continuous learning loop building on the progress already made and positioning teachers and leaders for sustained growth.

Bonus Resources: For a downloadable copy of the *Planning Tool for Year Two and Beyond*, please visit www.myedresource.com.

The bottom line is that Phase 5 transforms the *Follow Me Forward* experience into lasting momentum. The first group of teachers who have completed a learning loop will begin a second learning loop by reflecting, refining, and deepening their practice while adjusting their beliefs and values through lived experience. At the same time, a new group of teachers will begin their initial learning loop through five phases of the Follow Me Forward Model.

For example, a first loop led by one Host Teacher per grade level in kindergarten, first, and second grades with literacy goals may expand in the Year Two loop to include additional Host Teachers from those same grade levels (K, 1, and 2)—creating greater depth and consistency across early literacy practices.

In a middle school setting, the first loop might begin with a group of ELA teachers focused on increasing student talk through accountable discussion routines. In the Year Two loop, Exceptional Children teachers join in, and build capacity with the same goals so the inclusion work increases the practices exponentially within the ELA classrooms.

At the high school level, a first loop may start with English teachers exploring strategies for analyzing complex texts. In the Year Two Loop, those same teachers continue refining their craft while mentoring a new group of Host Teachers who teach history. The history teachers also explore strategies for analyzing complex texts in their area of content.

This intentional spiraling of learning loops ensures that professional learning is never a one-time event. Instead, it becomes an ongoing, collaborative rhythm within the life of the school. This promotes a culture where the values of lifelong learning, authenticity, and belonging continually shape and strengthen the beliefs of curiosity, collaboration, and meaning.

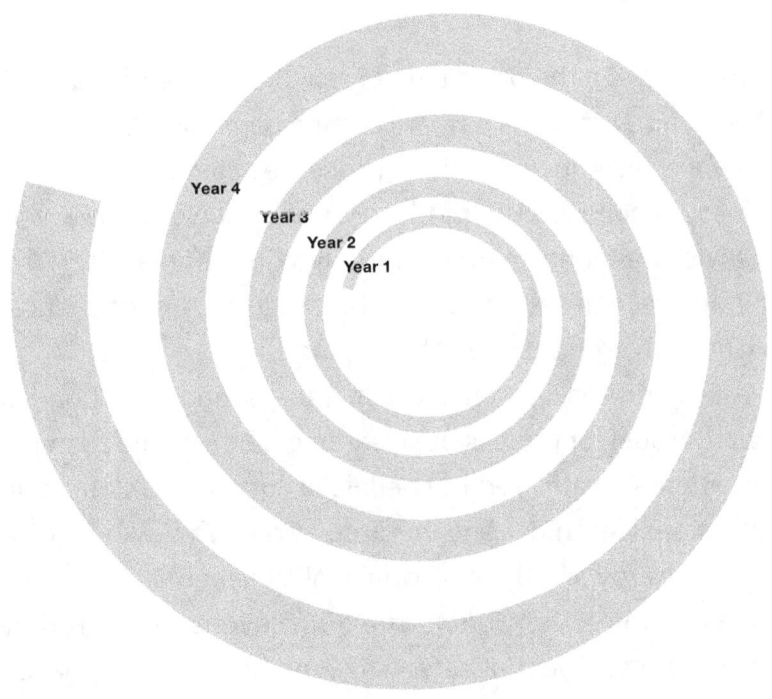

Elementary Case Study: Franklin Elementary School

Reflecting on the first year of the Follow Me Forward Model at the elementary level, the principal described the host classroom as a transformative addition to the school's professional learning culture:

"Having a Follow Me Forward classroom at the Elementary School has been incredibly beneficial for our teachers and students. Ms Hardy, the teacher leading this classroom, continues to stay current with best practices and receives ongoing training in math. What I love most is that her expertise doesn't just impact the students in her classroom; it reaches exponentially more.

When other teachers observe her in action and return to their classrooms to implement what they've learned, that's when the real ripple effect happens. They get to see Ms. Hardy navigate real-time challenges and witness how she differentiates instruction, meeting the needs of students who are struggling, on grade level, or ready for enrichment. They then spend time debriefing with her about their observations, and she explains what she has learned and why she made certain professional decisions during the lesson.

We are fully committed to doing whatever it takes to support student learning, and this Host Classroom is clearly making a powerful difference for all learners. We are proud and grateful to be part of it."

By the end of the first year, the principal at Franklin Elementary accepted a new position within the district. Ms. Hardy remains a Host Teacher, beginning another learning loop in Year Two with the confidence, insight, and refined processes gained from her inaugural year. This proves the model is sustainable, as the model did not dissolve when the principal took a new position, unlike many professional learning initiatives in schools. Ms. Hardy took pride in her role as an educator and recognized the value she brings to the teachers she works with and which develops a true and strong sense of belonging.

Additionally, the new principal at Franklin Elementary school is on board and is excited about the Follow Me Forward Model for professional learning. She jumped right in and discussed with Ms. Hardy how the experience affected the beliefs of curiosity, collaboration, and meaning in the context of professional learning. She inquired about what went well and the challenges with the five phases. Ms Hardy and the new principal also made time to sit with the first-grade team to look at data and mark the *Making the Shift* inventory in preparation to extend an invitation to begin an inaugural year of a learning loop through five phases as Host Teachers.

Middle School Case Study: West End Middle School

At the end of the learning loop, both Ms. Salinas and Ms. Morrigan committed to continue the following year. They felt the value of the work had changed not only what they do, but who they are as professionals. They were willing to continue, and they wanted to expand their small-group methods into additional classes. There was no need to coax or incentivize them into continuing to learn and lead from the classroom.

Ms. Salinas talked about the experience as transformational. "I came into this wanting to help my students by learning more about them. In the process, I learned more about myself, and in the end, I am a different teacher." Ms. Salinas continues in Year 2 of the work with an expansion. She wants to add more small groups across her week and increase the number of classes she works with in this way.

Ms. Morrigan felt a sense of purpose and renewal as she reflected on the work. She was finishing a graduate degree that could take her out of the classroom entirely. Because of the Follow Me Forward work, she had a spark for professional learning, loved being an instructional leader from her very own classroom, and naturally set goals for Year 2.

"Explaining what I do and how I do it to visitors was one of my favorite things about this project. It helped me think through why I do the things I do and also help other teachers," Ms. Morrigan said. "That feels good. We need each other and talking through ideas on what works and what doesn't was so helpful. I wish I had been able to visit a Host Teacher when I was trying to figure things out."

Preliminary testing data showed that students were proficient and able to demonstrate growth on end-of-year assessments. With insight and guidance from the Support Leader and principal, both Ms. Salinas and Ms. Morrigan continue to replicate the work in Year 2. As a result of the visits, new teachers committed to participating in the model and will also become Host Teachers by the end of the Year 2 work.

High School Case Study: Bailey High School

At the high school, Ms. Carmen and Ms. Woods reflected together on what worked and how their perceptions had shifted across the project. Each of them shared shifts in perspectives, but in different ways. Ms. Carmen thought she was getting into the professional learning project to learn more about assessment practices, which happened. In addition to that, she shared how she benefitted from the intentionality of the support sessions with the Continuum of Practice and how that also led her to be more aware of her own instructional choices.

"Having people visit is fun because it helps you see things you forgot you were doing. It is validating and rewarding to allow others to learn through observing."

Her authenticity put people at ease, so they could honestly collaborate and be curious. Several of the visitors from her group will move into the Host Teacher positions in the following year.

Ms. Woods continued to work with students on the assessment work and through professional conversations, shared deep reflections about teaching and learning. She shared how much she loved her relationships with her students and wanted to use that as a foundation for the work next year. Still in the Expansion stage, Ms. Woods has a clear starting point for the work in the coming year and can hit the ground running thanks to the foundation she created in year one of Follow Me Forward.

Bailey High School experienced some shifts at the end of the year due to district-level changes. Despite multiple setbacks, they are committed to forging ahead with professional learning. The principal knows the value of the Follow Me Forward Model for professional learning and will continue the work because he is also committed to lifelong learning. He was part of the reflective work and helped participants consider their shifts across the year. Once the staffing is complete, he will select a new school level Support Leader, and they will begin Phase 1 for the second year participants. This is one more example of how Follow Me Forward is sustainable even when there are shifts in staffing. The Host Teachers from Year 1 are able to lead from the classroom in a way that was not possible prior to the experience.

Summary

In Phase 5, teachers and leaders pause to reflect on what they've learned, how their beliefs have shifted, and how those changes will shape future practice. This phase marks a pivotal point where teachers and support leaders can end with reflection or continue forward into ongoing, embedded learning. *Follow Me Forward* embraces this continuous path, where professional growth evolves into a living culture within the school.

Teachers revisit the *Making the Shift* inventory, examine what worked and what challenged them, and commit to next steps. From here, the journey loops forward with experienced Host Teachers deepening their practice while teachers new to the project begin a Year 1 learning loop. This process ensures professional learning is sustained, collaborative, and always in motion.

Conclusion

Cultural Change:
The Lasting Impact of *Follow Me Forward*

The Follow Me Forward Model can generate more than improved instruction. It creates a ripple effect of cultural transformation. At its core, *Follow Me Forward* initiates cultural change at the school level, teacher level and student level. The shift in mindsets, beliefs, and practices profoundly influence the fabric of a school community. It moves professional learning from an isolated event to an embedded way of life.

Teacher Impact

- ◆ Strengthens instructional strategies/teacher effectiveness
- ◆ Increases confidence and self-efficacy
- ◆ Develops a willingness to receive feedback
- ◆ Encourages teachers to seek and use support

Follow Me Forward Model for Professional Learning

School Impact

- ◆ Creates a culture focused on learning
- ◆ Establishes an effective teacher collaboration
- ◆ Develops teacher leaders
- ◆ Reduces teacher burnout
- ◆ Supports teacher recruitment and retention

Student Impact

- ◆ Increases student engagement and collaboration
- ◆ Creates a willingness to learn from mistakes
- ◆ Develops higher-order thinking
- ◆ Improves student achievement

School Change

Follow Me Forward cultivates a schoolwide culture of learning. It replaces top-down directives with collaborative ecosystems where teachers are leaders and learning is everyone's responsibility. Schools that embrace Follow Me Forward experience curiosity and growth as cultural norms, teacher collaboration as a natural rhythm, and peer-led leadership as a sustaining force. Retention strengthens, burnout decreases, and shared beliefs emerge. Reflection and feedback are no longer compliance tasks but instead authentic tools for growth. The school itself becomes a living community of learners.

Teacher Change

Teachers are at the heart of *Follow Me Forward*. Rather than being passive recipients of professional learning, they become active cocreators of learning. *Follow Me Forward* honors their voice, choice, and professionalism. It leads to instructional growth, confidence, and renewed joy in teaching. Teachers begin to expect and value feedback, seek support, and contribute to one another's success. This shift restores the authenticity of teaching because it reminds educators that their work is not about programs to be implemented, but about people growing together.

Student Change

When educators thrive, students thrive. *Follow Me Forward* can build classrooms where learning is collaborative, reflective and rigorous. As teachers live out the values of lifelong learning and authenticity, students see those values modeled and mirrored. They learn that growth is not about perfection but about progress. They see that feedback fuels learning and that collaboration strengthens understanding. The result is heightened engagement, deeper critical thinking, and authentic academic achievement.

Final Thoughts

Ultimately, *Follow Me Forward* nurtures a culture where lifelong learning is expected, authenticity is honored, and belonging is felt by all. It fosters environments where curiosity drives growth, collaboration builds strength, and meaningful work sustains motivation.

At the intersection of school, teacher, and student change lies the true power of *Follow Me Forward*. It is a transformational process that restores humanity to professional learning. Our schools and classrooms are not full of numbers. They are full of people and Jane from our introduction is alive and real. *Follow Me Forward* is a professional learning model that reframes our shared responsibility and repositions it as the heart of cultural change in our schools. Cultural change does not occur by mandate. It happens when educators like Jane are invited to learn, lead, and grow together with quality support in place. This is when professional learning becomes not a requirement, but a way of being.

As the cultural diagram illustrates, *Follow Me Forward* is not a program to be implemented. It is a living process of transformation. It reshapes the mindset around professional learning, elevates teaching practice and renews school culture. It is, at its essence, a movement toward schools where curiosity is celebrated, collaboration is embraced, and meaning is found in the daily work of teaching and learning together.

Follow Me Forward prioritizes humans over metrics and products because lasting change begins with people. When we centralize and honor the humans within the work, educators feel seen, valued, and connected, and authentic growth naturally follows.

This is the cultural change we need in schools today.

This is *Follow Me Forward*.

Bonus Resource - Follow Me Forward Testimonials www.myedresource.com

Appendices

Appendix 1. Follow Me Forward Roles

Roles in the Follow Me Forward Model

Support Leaders	ERG	Host Teachers	Visitors (Phases 4 and 5)
• Lead with a shared vision for FMF • Clearly explain the support process: one demo followed by three support sessions • Provide written and oral feedback in three support sessions • Review and reflect on feedback given to the host teacher • Stay focused on goals • Reinforce that FMF is supportive, not evaluative • Ask clarifying questions as needed • Set goals collaboratively for each learning loop • Be responsive and supportive of Host Teachers • Consider next steps as the learning loop concludes	• Lead with a shared vision • Be available to Support Leaders between visits to campus (phone calls etc) • Capture the learning and summarize each campus visit for the school • Debrief with admin/point of contact throughout the five phases of FMF • Offer expert and responsive resources and tips as needed • Stay focused on project goals and Support Leader • Help Support Leaders collaboratively with host teachers • Be responsive and supportive	• Be open to coaching and new learning • Plan ahead for the support session • Attend debrief sessions • Use feedback for growth • Apply provided resources and strategies • Collaborate on goal-setting with Support Leader • Communicate professionally • Engage in honest reflection and dialogue • Plan ahead and set dates for visitors (three visits)	• Open to learning • Stay focused • Understand the role within the larger picture of the project • Actively engage in the debrief sessions • Remain curious and reflect on next steps

Appendix 2.
Continuum of Practice Sample

Continuum of Practice

Goals:

1. *Make a shift toward teaching more often in small groups—reducing whole-group instruction.*
2. *Increase opportunities for productive small-group learning in ELA.*

Foundation Stage	
Student Indicators	• Students can sometimes sustain independent work on meaningful, manageable tasks. • Students begin to problem-solve issues with some success.
Teacher Indicators	• The teacher establishes and demonstrates clear processes and procedures. • The teacher clarifies expectations for independent time. • The teacher models routines and provides guidance and feedback as students build stamina.
Notes and Reflections	

Expansion Stage	
Student Indicators	• Students sustain independent work for a minimum of 20 minutes. • Students transition smoothly through rotations. • Students use materials and resources productively. • Students problem-solve issues independently of the teacher.
Teacher Indicators	(for small groups) • The teacher forms small groups based on relevant data. • The teacher sets a clear, standards-aligned purpose for lessons. • The teacher provides targeted feedback related to the purpose. • The teacher notices and records student thinking. • The teacher begins analyzing notes to consider next steps. • The teacher usually releases most of the time to students for learning while observing their thinking.
Notes and Reflections	

Refinement Stage
Includes all indicators from the Foundation and Expansion stages, plus the following

Student Indicators	• Students demonstrate consistent high engagement and quality output. • Students use a wide variety of texts (fiction, nonfiction, poetry, articles, etc.). • Student-to-student dialogue increases. • Students regularly reflect and set personal goals.
Teacher Indicators	• The teacher consistently uses multiple data sources to plan and flex groups (not only at assessment times). • The teacher maintains a systematic record-keeping process for notes. • The teacher articulates patterns from student thinking to plan next steps. • The teacher models teacher thinking transparently. • The teacher gives effective feedback to students that moves learning forward. • The teacher facilitates high-level, purposeful conversations aligned with standards and academic vocabulary. • The teacher responsively adjusts instruction based on what is learned during the lesson.
Notes and Reflections	

Lesson Snapshot & Goals

Appendix 3.
Continuum of Practice with Feedback

Continuum of Practice

Observed Indicator= ☑

Goals:

1. *Make a shift toward teaching more often in small groups—reducing whole-group instruction.*
2. *Increase opportunities for productive small-group learning in ELA.*

Foundation Stage	
Student Indicators	• Students can sometimes sustain independent work on meaningful, manageable tasks. ☑ • Students begin to problem-solve issues with some success. ☑
Teacher Indicators	• The teacher establishes and demonstrates clear processes and procedures. • The teacher clarifies expectations for independent time. • The teacher models routines and provides guidance and feedback as students build stamina.
Notes and Reflections	*Tip: You were interrupted by the classroom phone. Can you assign a student to answer?*

Expansion Stage	
Student Indicators	• Students sustain independent work for a minimum of 20 minutes. • Students transition smoothly through rotations. ☑ • Students use materials and resources productively. ☑ • Students problem-solve issues independently of the teacher.

Teacher Indicators	(for small groups)
	• The teacher forms small groups based on relevant data. ☑
	• The teacher sets a clear, standards-aligned purpose for lessons.
	
	   using mental images to make inferences
	
	• The teacher provides targeted feedback related to the purpose.
	• The teacher notices and records student thinking. ☑
	• The teacher begins analyzing notes to consider next steps.
	• The teacher usually releases most of the time to students for learning while observing their thinking.
	   released students to read the poem on their own

Notes and Reflections	*You were able to notice that students are not used to being held accountable for high-quality work.* *Reflect: How can you give feedback to raise awareness around quality?*

Refinement Stage *Includes all indicators from the Foundation and Expansion stages, plus the following*	
Student Indicators	• Students demonstrate consistent high engagement and quality output. • Students use a wide variety of texts (fiction, nonfiction, poetry, articles, etc.). ✅ • Student-to-student dialogue increases. • Students regularly reflect and set personal goals.
Teacher Indicators	• The teacher consistently uses multiple data sources to plan and flex groups (not only at assessment times). • The teacher maintains a systematic record-keeping process for notes. ✅ • The teacher articulates patterns from student thinking to plan next steps. • The teacher models teacher thinking transparently. ✅ • The teacher gives effective feedback to students that moves learning forward. • The teacher facilitates high-level, purposeful conversations aligned with standards and academic vocabulary. • The teacher responsively adjusts instruction based on what is learned during the lesson.
Notes and Reflections	*Tip: Remind students that conversation can help increase understanding. The more they practice talking, the easier it will become.* *Reflect: Based on what you noticed, what will you adjust?*

Lesson Snapshot & Goals

The small group continues to reveal student thinking. This is valuable because you are identifying gaps in real time and considering ways to support with instruction.

Goals:

1. Explicitly state and model a clear purpose.

2. Consider which groups need the practice on just visualizing and which groups can handle visualization to make an inference.

3. I am sending you a support resource for making inferences. You can decide if and how you use it.

Appendix 4. Collaborative Debrief Tool

Collaborative Debrief Tool

To guide a reflective, two-way conversation after a lesson.

	Support Leader Brings	**Host Teacher Brings**
Stance & Focus	• A stance of curiosity, not judgment—asking probing questions to understand the teacher's perspective. • Noticings about student engagement, pacing, and alignment with intended goals. • Affirmation that validates the teacher's self-assessment and learning. **Sample Questions:** – What part of the lesson felt most alive to you? – What surprised you about student responses?	• Honest reflection about what worked and what surprised them. • Evidence of student engagement or learning (student work samples, comments, or observed behaviors). • Awareness of emotional and instructional moments that stood out during the lesson.
Goal Connection & Clarification	• Connection back to the goal set in the Continuum of Learning. • Prompts that unpack the learning intention (e.g., "What thinking did you hope to see?"). • Clarifying questions to help identify the targeted skill, strategy, or behavior. **Sample Questions:** – What thinking did you hope to see? – How did you communicate the goal to students? – What did you notice students doing that reflected progress toward the goal?	• Description of how the goal was communicated to students. • Reflections on whether students met expectations or need additional scaffolding.

	Support Leader Brings	**Host Teacher Brings**
Interpretation & Guidance	• Encouragement to interpret student evidence rather than evaluate teaching. • Curiosity about what the teacher noticed in the moment. • Guidance that connects observations to next instructional steps. **Sample Questions:** – What patterns do you see in student responses? – How do these insights inform what comes next? – What might you adjust or keep the same next time?	• Specific examples of what students said, did, or produced. • Insights into student readiness, engagement, or misconceptions. • Reflection on how these insights might shape upcoming instruction.
Next Steps & Support	• One actionable suggestion aligned with the teacher's goal. • Offer of support—resources, modeling, or collaboration if requested. **Sample Questions:** – What do you see as your next action step? – What kind of support feels most useful right now?	• Personal takeaway or small action step for continued growth. • Reflections on what support or feedback would be most helpful moving forward.

Appendix 5.
What the Visit Is / What the Visit Is Not

What the Visit to the Host Classroom Is	What the Visit to the Host Classroom Is Not
A time to learn from a peer	Letting your peer know what they did well and what they need to improve
Time to be a part of a schoolwide culture of curiosity, collaboration, and meaning	Expecting a perfect result from the lesson
A process for better understanding students and how to meet their needs	Passing blame on students or others when lessons are not perfect
A journey to continually improve one's teaching practice	Self-assessing one's or others worth as a teacher
An opportunity to engage in experiential professional learning	A chance to get out of teaching in your classroom

References Cited

Anderson, D. L. 2020. *Organization Development: The Process of Leading Organizational Change* (5th ed.). SAGE.

Brookfield, S. D. 1995. *Becoming a Critically Reflective Teacher*. Jossey-Bass.

Brookfield, S. D. 2017. *Becoming a Critically Reflective Teacher* (2nd ed.). Jossey-Bass.

Brown, B. 2010. *The Gifts of Imperfection: Let Go of Who You Think You're Supposed to Be and Embrace Who You Are*. Hazelden Publishing.

Cambourne, B. Why a Teacher's Belief Matter: Using A Theory of Learning to Explore Instructional Decisions Fall 2022 - *The Journal of Reading Recovery* 22 (1)

Cells, P., Sabina, L. L., Touchton, D., Shankar-Brown, R., & Sabina, K. L. 2023. "Addressing teacher retention within the first three to five years of employment." *The Athens Journal of Education* 10 (2): 345–364. https://doi.org/10.30958/aje.10-2-9

Connor, C. M., Piasta, S. B., & Zhou, Y. 2024. "Coaching for deeper learning: The role of sustained support." *Journal of Teacher Education* 75 (3): 278–295.

Crouch, D. 2022. "Why a teacher's beliefs matter: Using a theory of learning to explore instructional decisions." *Journal of Reading Recovery* Fall, 2022 issue.

Deci, E. I., & Ryan, R. M. 2000. "The "what" and "why" of goal pursuits: Human needs and the self-determination of behavior." *Psychological Inquiry* 11 (4): 227–268. https://doi.org/10.1207/S15327965PLI1104_01

Gore, J., Miller, A., Fray, L., Harris, J., & Taggart, W. 2024. "Quality teaching rounds: A randomized controlled trial." *Teaching and Teacher Education* 129, 104126.

Harvard Graduate School of Education. (2023, January 23). *Turning around teacher turnover*. Usable Knowledge. https://www.gse.harvard.edu/ideas/usable-knowledge/23/01/turning-around-teacher-turnover

Hill, H. C., & Papay, J. P. 2025. "Professional development and instructional improvement: A meta-analysis." *Educational Researcher* 54 (2): 123–137.

Knowles, M. S. 1984. *The Adult Learner: A Neglected Species* (3rd ed.). Gulf Publishing.

Knowles, M. S., Holton, E. F., & Swanson, R. A. 2015. *The Adult Learner: The Definitive Classic in Adult Education and Human Resource Development* (8th ed.). Routledge.

Kolb, D. A. 1984. *Experiential Learning: Experience as the Source of Learning and Development*. Prentice Hall.

Laird, L. D., Bloom-Feshbach, K., McNamara, T., Gibbs, B., & Pololi, L. H. 2024, June. "Psychological safety: Creating a transformative culture in a faculty group peer-mentoring intervention." *Chronicle of Mentoring & Coaching* 8 (1): 127–140. https://doi.org/10.62935/hz7383

Lewin, K. 1947. "Frontiers in group dynamics." *Human Relations* 1 (1): 5–41. https://doi.org/10.1177/001872674700100103

Mezirow, J. 1991. *Transformative Dimensions of Adult Learning*. Jossey-Bass.

Mezirow, J., & Taylor, E. W. (Eds.). 2009. *Transformative Learning in Practice: Insights from Community, Workplace, and Higher Education*. Jossey-Bass.

Nguyen, T. D., Lam, C. B., & Bruno, P. 2024. What do we know about the extent of teacher shortages nationwide? A systematic examination of reports of U.S. teacher shortages. AERA Open.

Pink, D. H. 2009. *Drive: The Surprising Truth about What Motivates Us*. Riverhead Books.

Powers, W. T. 1973. *Behavior: The Control of Perception*. Aldine.

Powers, W. T. 2005. *Behavior: The Control of Perception* (2nd ed.). Benchmark Publications.

Rhodes, M., & Melville, C. (2024, May 1). Taking Risks with Rough Draft Teaching. *Educational Leadership, 81*(8).

TNTP. 2015. *The Mirage: Confronting the hard truth about our quest for teacher development*. TNTP.https://tntp.org/publication/the-mirage-confronting-the-truth-about-our-quest-for-teacher-development

Vygotsky, L. S. 1978. *Mind in Society: The Development of Higher Psychological Processes*. Harvard University Press.

About the Authors

Hope Reagan

Hope received her bachelor's degree in elementary education from The University of North Carolina at Greensboro. Her educational experience includes elementary, middle, and high school instruction with both students and teachers. Hope has worked with a national research lab in analyzing best practices for reading assessments. She earned her master's degree in language and literacy from Salem College and is certified to teach reading and writing in grades K–12. Hope can be reached at hope@myedresource.com.

Alice Oakley

Alice received her bachelor's degree in early and middle grades education from Radford University. Her educational experience includes elementary, middle and high school instruction. As a National Board Certified Teacher, she has worked with both students and teachers on instruction and human behavior. She earned a Master of Education degree in Curriculum and Instruction from The University of North Carolina at Greensboro. In addition, she earned a K–12 reading certification and recently completed a Master of Human Resource Development from Clemson University with a concentration in Learning Leadership. Alice can be reached at alice@myedresource.com.

Hope and Alice are dedicated to growing all learners. They are available for speaking engagements, ongoing coaching support, content creation, consultations, and resource development. Stay in touch by signing up on their website www.myedresource.com.

www.ingramcontent.com/pod-product-compliance
Lightning Source LLC
Chambersburg PA
CBHW081535120626
46550CB00009B/2743